The Cambridge Manuals of Science and Literature

THE IDEA OF GOD

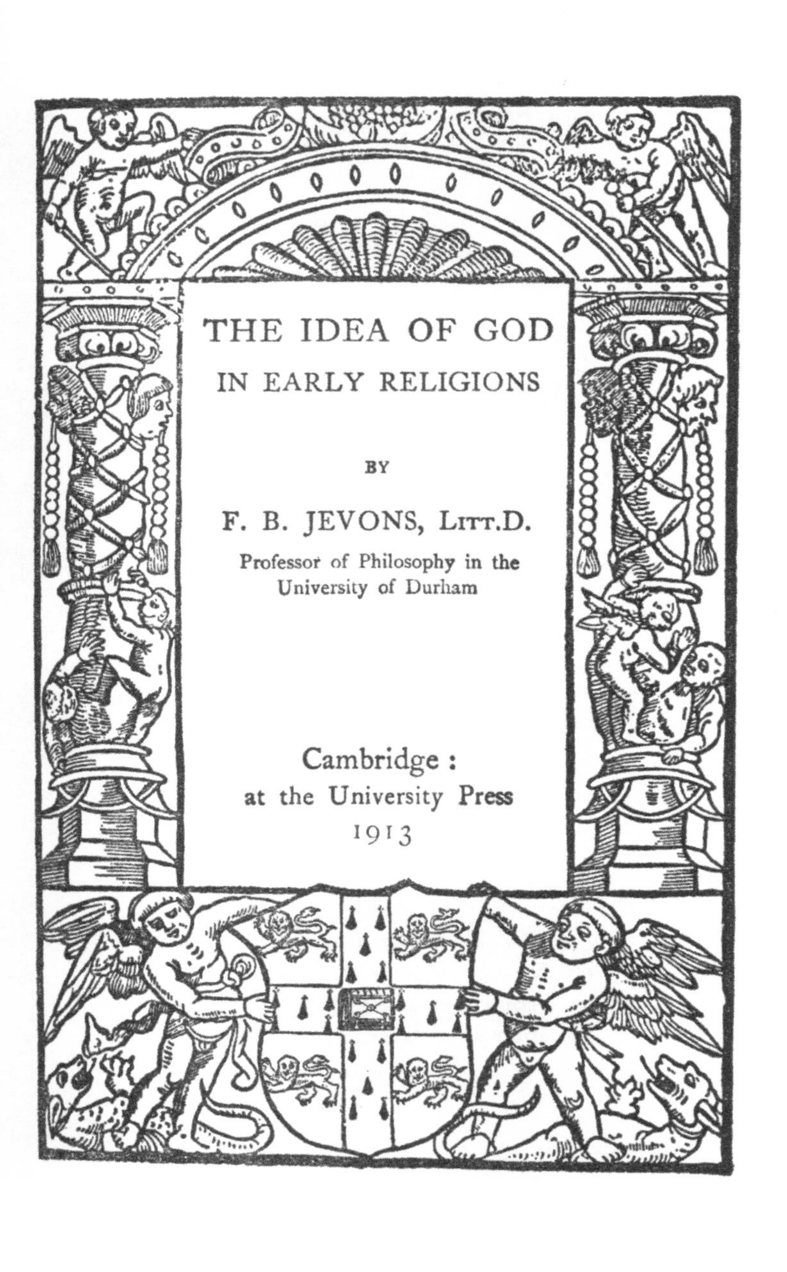

THE IDEA OF GOD IN EARLY RELIGIONS

BY

F. B. JEVONS, Litt.D.
Professor of Philosophy in the
University of Durham

Cambridge:
at the University Press
1913

CAMBRIDGE UNIVERSITY PRESS
Cambridge, New York, Melbourne, Madrid, Cape Town,
Singapore, São Paulo, Delhi, Tokyo, Mexico City

Cambridge University Press
The Edinburgh Building, Cambridge CB2 8RU, UK

Published in the United States of America by Cambridge University Press, New York

www.cambridge.org
Information on this title: www.cambridge.org/9781107634602

First published 1910
Reprinted 1911, 1913
First paperback edition 2011

A catalogue record for this publication is available from the British Library

ISBN 978-1-107-63460-2 Paperback

With the exception of the coat of arms at the foot, the design on the title page is a reproduction of one used by the earliest known Cambridge printer John Siberch 1521

PREFACE

IN *The Varieties of Religious Experience* the late Professor William James has said (p. 465): 'The religious phenomenon, studied as an inner fact, and apart from ecclesiastical or theological complications, has shown itself to consist everywhere, and at all its stages, in the consciousness which individuals have of an intercourse between themselves and higher powers with which they feel themselves to be related. This intercourse is realised at the time as being both active and mutual.' The book now before the reader deals with the religious phenomenon, studied as an inner fact, in the earlier stages of religion. By 'the Idea of God' may be meant either the consciousness which individuals have of higher powers, with which they feel themselves to be related, or the words in which they, or others, seek to express that consciousness. Those words may be an expression, that is to say an interpretation or a misinterpretation, of that consciousness. But the words are not the consciousness: the feeling, without which the consciousness does not exist, may be absent when the words are spoken or heard. It is however through the words that we have to approach the feeling and the consciousness of others, and to determine whether and how far the feeling and the consciousness so approached are similar in all individuals everywhere and at all stages.

F. B. JEVONS.

HATFIELD HALL,
DURHAM.
October, 1910

CONTENTS

BIBLIOGRAPHY

Allen, Grant. The Evolution of the Idea of God. London, 1897.
Anthropology and the Classics. Oxford, 1908.
Bastian, A. Volks- und Menschenkunde. Berlin, 1888.
Bousset, W. What is Religion? (English Translation). London, 1907.
Crawley, A. E. The Idea of the Soul. London, 1909.
Fossey, C. La Magie Assyrienne. Paris, 1902.
Frazer, J. G. Early History of the Kingship. London, 1895.
—— The Golden Bough. London, 1900.
—— Psyche's Task. London, 1909.
Gardner, P. Modernity and the Churches. London, 1909.
Hobhouse, L. T. Morals in Evolution. London, 1906.
Höffding, H. The Philosophy of Religion (English Translation). London, 1906.
Hollis, A. C. The Masai. Oxford, 1905.
—— The Nandi. Oxford, 1909.
James, W. The Varieties of Religious Experience. London, 1902.
Jastrow, M. Jun. Study of Religion. London, 1901.
Jevons, F. B. Introduction to the History of Religion. London, 1896.
—— Religion in Evolution. London, 1906.
—— Study of Comparative Religion. London, 1908.
Lang, A. Magic and Religion. London, 1901.
—— The Making of Religion. London, 1898.

Mackenzie, W. D. The Final Faith. London, 1910.
Marett, R. R. The Threshold of Religion. London, 1909.
Mitchell, H. B. Talks on Religion. London, 1908.
Nassau, R. H. Fetichism in West Africa. London, 1904.
Parker, K. L. The Euahlayi Tribe. London, 1905.
Saussaye, P. D. C. de la. Religionsgeschichte. Freiburg i. B., 1889.
Schaarschmidt, C. Die Religion. Leipzig, 1907.
Thompson, R. C. Semitic Magic. London, 1908.
Tisdall, W. St C. Comparative Religion. London, 1909.
Transactions of the Third International Congress of the History of Religions. Oxford, 1908.
Tylor, E. B. Primitive Culture. London, 1873.
Westermarck, E. Origin and Development of Moral Ideas. London, 1906.
Wundt, W. Völkerpsychologie. Leipzig, 1904—6.

I

INTRODUCTION

Every child that is born is born of a community and into a community, which existed before his birth and will continue to exist after his death. He learns to speak the language which the community spoke before he was born, and which the community will continue to speak after he has gone. In learning the language he acquires not only words but ideas; and the words and ideas he acquires, the thoughts he thinks and the words in which he utters them, are those of the community from which he learnt them, which taught them before he was born and will go on teaching them after he is dead. He not only learns to speak the words and think the ideas, to reproduce the mode of thought, as he does the form of speech, of the circumambient community: he is taught and learns to act as those around him do—as the community has done and will tend to do. The community —the narrower community of the family, first, and, afterwards, the wider community to which the family belongs—teaches him how he ought to speak, what he ought to think, and how he ought to act. The consciousness of the child reproduces the consciousness of the community to which he belongs—the common consciousness, which existed before him and will continue to exist after him.

The common consciousness is not only the source from which the individual gets his mode of speech, thought and action, but the court of appeal which decides what is fact. If a question is raised whether the result of a scientific experiment is what it is alleged by the original maker of the experiment to be, the appeal is to the common consciousness: any one who chooses to make the experiment in the way described will find the result to be of the kind alleged; if everyone else, on experiment, finds it to be so, it is established as a fact of common consciousness; if no one else finds it to be so, the alleged discovery is not a fact but an erroneous inference.

Now, it is not merely with regard to external facts or facts apprehended through the senses, that the common consciousness is accepted as the court of appeal. The allegation may be that an emotion, of a specified kind—alarm or fear, wonder or awe—is, in specified circumstances, experienced as a fact of the common consciousness. Or a body of men may have a common purpose, or a common idea, as well as an emotion of, say, common alarm. If the purpose, idea or emotion, be common to them and experienced by all of them, it is a fact of their common consciousness. In this case, as in the case of any alleged but disputed discovery in science, the common consciousness is the court of appeal which decides the facts, and determines whether what an individual thinks he has discovered in his consciousness is really a fact of the common consciousness. The idea of powers superior to man, the emotion of awe or reverence, which goes with the idea, and the purpose of communicating with the power in question are facts, not peculiar to this or that individual consciousness, but facts of the common consciousness of all mankind.

The child up to a certain age has no consciousness of self: the absence of self-consciousness is one of the charms of children. The child imitates its elders, who speak of him and to him by his name. He speaks of himself in the third person and not in the first person singular, and designates himself by his proper name and not by means of the personal pronoun 'I'; eventually the child acquires the use and to some extent learns the meaning of the first personal pronoun; that is, if the language of the community to which he belongs has developed so far as to have produced such a pronoun. For there was a period in the evolution of speech when, as yet, a first personal pronoun had not been evolved; and that, probably, for the simple reason that the idea which it denotes was as unknown to the community as it is to the child whose absence of self-consciousness is so pleasing. For a period, the length of which may have been millions of years, the common consciousness, the consciousness of the community, did not discover or discriminate, in language or in thought, the existence of the individual self.

The importance of this consideration lies in its bearing upon the question, in what form the idea of powers superior to man disclosed itself in the common consciousness at that period. It is held by many students of the science of religion that fetishism preceded polytheism in the history of religion; and it is undoubted that polytheism flourished at the expense of fetishism. But what is exactly the difference between fetishism and polytheism? No one now any longer holds that a fetish is regarded, by believers in fetish, as a material object and nothing more: everyone recognises that the material object to which the term is applied is regarded as the habitation of a spiritual being. The material object in question is to the fetish what the idol of a god is to a god. If the material object, through which, or in which, the fetish-spirit manifests itself, bears no resemblance to human form, neither do the earliest stocks or blocks in which gods manifest themselves bear any resemblance to human form.

Such unshaped stocks do not of themselves tell us whether they are fetishes or gods to their worshippers. The test by which the student of the science of religion determines the question is a very simple one: it is, who worships the object in question? If the object is the private property of some individual, it is fetish; if it is worshipped by the community as a whole, it, or rather the spirit which manifests itself therein, is a god of the community. The functions of the two beings differ accordingly: the god receives the prayers of the community and has power to grant them; the fetish has power to grant the wishes of the individual who owns it. The consequence of this difference in function is that as the wishes of the individual may be inconsistent with the welfare of other members of the community; as the fetish may be, and actually is, used to procure injury and death to other members of the community; a fetish is anti-social and a danger to the community, whereas a god of the community is there expressly as a refuge and a help for the community. The fetish fulfils the desires of the individual, the self; the god listens to the prayers of the community.

Let us now return to that stage in the evolution of the community when, as yet, neither the language nor the thought of the community had discovered or discriminated the existence of the individual self. If at that stage there was in the common consciousness any idea, however dim or confused, of powers superior to man; if that idea was accompanied or coloured by any emotion, whether of fear or awe or reverence; if that emotion prompted action of any kind; then, such powers were not conceived to be fetishes, for the function of a fetish is to fulfil the desires of an individual self; and until the existence of the individual self is realised, there is no function for a fetish to perform.

It may well be that the gradual development of self-consciousness, and the slow steps by which language helped to bring forth the idea of self, were from the first, and throughout, accompanied by the gradual development of the idea of fetishism. But the very development of the idea of a power which could fulfil the desires of self, as distinguished from, and often opposed to, the interests of the community, would stimulate the growth of the idea of a power whose special and particular function was to tend the interests of the community as a whole. Thus the idea of a fetish and the idea of a god could only persist on condition of becoming more and more inconsistent with, and contradictory of, one another. If the lines followed by the two ideas started from the same point, it was only to diverge the more, the further they were pursued. And the tendency of fetishism to disappear from the later and higher stages of religion is sufficient to show that it did not afford an adequate or satisfactory expression of the idea contained in the common consciousness of some power or being greater than man. That idea is constantly striving, throughout the history of religion, to find or give expression to itself; it is constantly discovering that such expressions as it has found for itself do it wrong; and it is constantly throwing, or in the process of throwing, such expressions aside. Fetishism was thrown aside sooner than polytheism: for it was an expression not only inadequate but contradictory to the idea that gave it birth. The emotions of fear and suspicion, with which the community regarded fetishes, were emotions different from the awe or reverence with which the community approached its gods.

What practically provokes and stimulates the individual's dawning consciousness of himself, or the community's consciousness of the individual as in a way distinct from itself, is the clash between the desires, wishes, interests of the one, and the desires, wishes and interests of the other. But though the interests of the one are sometimes at variance with those of the other, still in some cases, also, the interests of the individual—even though they be purely individual interests—are not inconsistent with those of the community; and in most cases they are identical with them—the individual promotes his own interests by serving those of the community, and promotes those of the community by serving his own. In a word, the interests of the one are not so clearly and plainly cut off from those of the other, that the individual can always be condemned for seeking to gratify his self-interests or his own personal desires. That is presumably one reason why fetishism is so wide-spread and so long-lived in Western Africa, for instance: though fetishes may be used for anti-social purposes, they may be and are also used for purposes which if selfish are not, or are not felt to be, anti-social. The individual owner of a fetish does not feel that his ownership does or ought to cut him off from membership of the community. And so long as such feeling is common, so long an indecisive struggle between gods and fetishes continues.

Now this same cause—the impossibility of condemning the individual for seeking to promote his own interests—will be found on examination to be operative elsewhere, viz. in magic. The relation of magic to religion is as much a matter of doubt and dispute as is that of fetishism to religion. And I propose to treat magic in much the same way as I have treated fetishism. The justification which I offer for so doing is to be found in the parallel or analogy that may be drawn between them. The distinction which comes to be drawn within the common consciousness between the self and the community manifests itself obviously in the fact that the interests and desires of the individual are felt to be different, and yet not to be different, from those of the community; and so they are felt to be, yet not to be, condemnable from the point of view of the common consciousness. Now, this is precisely the judgment which is passed upon magic, wherever it is cultivated. It is condemnable, it is viewed with suspicion, fear and condemnation; and yet it is also and at the same time viewed and practised with general approval. It may be used on behalf of the community and for the good of the community, and with public approval, as it is when it is used to make the rain which the community needs. It may be viewed with toleration, as it is when it is believed to benefit an individual without entailing injury on the community. But it is visited with condemnation, and perhaps with punishment, when it is employed for purposes, such as murder, which the common consciousness condemns. Accordingly the person who has the power to work the marvels comprehended under the name of magic is viewed with condemnation, toleration or approval, according as he uses his power for purposes which the common consciousness condemns, tolerates or approves. The power which such a person exerts is power personal to him; and yet it is in a way a power greater and other than himself, for he has it not always under his control or command: whether he uses it for the benefit of the community or for the injury of some individual, he cannot count on its always coming off. And this fact is not without its influence and consequences. If he is endeavouring to use it for the injury of some person, he will explain his failure as due to some error he has committed in the *modus operandi*, or to the counter-operations of some rival. But if he is endeavouring to exercise it for the benefit of the community, failure makes others doubtful whether he has the power to act on behalf of the community; while, on the contrary, a successful issue makes it clear that he has the power, and places him, in the opinion both of the community and of himself, in an exceptional position: his power is indeed in a way personal to himself, but it is also greater and other than himself. His sense of it, and the community's sense of it, is reinforced and augmented by the approval of the common consciousness, and by the feeling that a power, in harmony with the common consciousness and the community's desires, is working in him and through him. This power, thus exercised, of working marvels for the common good is obviously more closely analogous to that of a prophet working miracles, than it is to that of the witch working injury or death. And, in the same way that I have already suggested that gods and fetishes may have been evolved from a prior indeterminate concept, which was neither but might become either; so I would now suggest that miracles are not magic, nor is magic miracles, but that the two have been differentiated from a common source. And if the polytheistic gods, which are to be found where fetishism is believed in, present us with a very low stage in the development of the idea of a 'perfect personality,' so too the sort of miracles which are believed in, where the belief in magic flourishes, present us with a very low stage in the development of the idea of an almighty God. Axe-heads that float must have belonged originally to such a low stage; and rods that turn into serpents were the property of the 'magicians of Egypt' as well as of Aaron.

The common source, then, from which flows the power of working marvels for the community's good, or of working magic in the interest of one individual member and perhaps to the injury of another, is a personal power, which in itself—that is to say, apart from the intention with which it is used and apart from the consequences which ensue—is neither commendable nor condemnable from the community's point of view; and which consequently can neither be condemned nor commended by the common consciousness, until the difference between self and the community has become manifest, and the possibility of a divergence between the interests of self or *alter* and those of the community has been realised. Further, this power, in whichever way it comes to be exercised, marks a strong individuality; and may be the first, as it is certainly a most striking, manifestation of the fact of individuality: it marks off, at once, the individual possessing such power from the rest of the community. And the common consciousness is puzzled by the apparition. Just as it tolerates fetishes though it disapproves of them and is afraid of them, so it tolerates the magician, though it is afraid of him and does not cordially approve of him, even when he benefits an individual client without injuring the community. But though the man of power may use, and apparently most often does use, his power, in the interest of some individual and to the detriment of the community; and though it is this condemnable use which is everywhere most conspicuous, and probably earliest developed; still there is no reason why he should not use, and as a matter of fact he sometimes does use, his power on behalf of the community to promote the food-supply of the community or to produce the rain which is desired. In this case, then, the individual, having a power which others have not, is not at variance with the community but in harmony with the common consciousness, and becomes an organ by which it acts. When, then, the belief in gods, having the interests of the community at heart, presents itself or develops within the common consciousness, the individual who has the power on behalf of the community to make rain or increase the food supply is marked out by the belief of the community—or it may be by the communings of his own heart—as specially related to the gods. Hence we find, in the low stages of the evolution of religion, the proceedings, by which the man of power had made rain for the community or increased the food-supply, either incorporated into the ritual of the gods, or surviving traditionally as incidents in the life of a prophet, e.g. the rain-making of Elijah. In the same way therefore as I have suggested that the resemblances between gods and fetishes are to be explained by the theory that the two go back to a common source, and that neither is developed from the other, so I suggest that the resemblances between the conception of prophet and that of magician point not to the priority of either to the other, but to the derivation or evolution of both from a prior and less determinate concept.

Just as a fetish is a material thing, and something more, so a magician is a man and something more. Just as a god is an idol and something more, so a prophet or priest is a man and something more. The fetish is a material thing which manifests a power that other things do not exhibit; and the magician is a man possessing a power which other men have not. The difference between the magician and the prophet or priest is the same as the difference between the fetish and the god. It is the difference between that which subserves the wishes of the individual, which may be, and often are, anti-social, and that which furthers the interests of the community. Of this difference each child who is born into the community learns from his elders: it is part of the common consciousness of the community. And it could not become a fact of the common consciousness until the existence of self became recognised in thought and expressed in language. With that recognition of difference, or possible difference, between the individual and the community, between the desires of the one and the welfare of the other, came the recognition of a difference between fetish and god, between magician and priest. The power exercised by either was greater than that of man; but the power manifested in the one was exercised with a view to the good of the community; in the case of the other, not. Thus, from the beginning, gods were not merely beings exercising power greater than that of man, but beings exercising their power for the good of man. It is as such that, from the beginning to the end, they have figured both in the common consciousness of the community, and in the consciousness of every member born into the community. They have figured in both; and, because they have figured both in the individual consciousness and the common consciousness, they have, from the beginning, been something present to both, something at once within the individual and without. But as the child recognises objects long before he becomes aware of the existence of himself, so man, in his infancy, sought this power or being in the external world long before he looked for it within himself.

It is because man looked for this being or power in the external world that he found, or thought he found, it there. He looked for it and found it, in the same way as to this day the African negro finds a fetish. A negro found a stone and took it for his fetish, as Professor Tylor relates, as follows:—'He was once going out on important business, but crossing the threshold he trod on this stone and hurt himself. Ha! ha! thought he, art thou there? So he took the stone, and it helped him through his undertaking for days.' So too when the community's attention is arrested by something in the external world, some natural phenomenon which is marvellous in their eyes, their attitude of mind, the attitude of the common consciousness, translated into words is: 'Ha! ha! art thou there?' This attitude of mind is one of expectancy: man finds a being, possessed of greater power than man's, because he is ready to find it and expecting it.

So strong is this expectancy, so ready is man to find this being, superior to man, that he finds it wherever he goes, wherever he looks. There is probably no natural phenomenon whatever that has not somewhere, at some time, provoked the question or the reflection 'Art thou there?' And it is because man has taken upon himself to answer the question, and to say: 'Thou art there, in the great and strong wind which rends the mountains; or, in the earthquake; or, in the fire' that polytheism has arisen. Perhaps, however, we should rather use the word 'polydaemonism' than 'polytheism.' By a god is usually meant a being who has come to possess a proper name; and, probably, a spirit is worshipped for some considerable time, before the appellative, by which he is addressed, loses its original meaning, and comes to be the proper name by which he, and he alone, is addressed. Certainly, the stage in which spirits without proper names are worshipped seems to be more primitive than that in which the being worshipped is a god, having a proper name of his own. And the difference between the two stages of polydaemonism and polytheism is not merely limited to the fact that the beings worshipped have proper names in the later stage, and had none in the earlier. A development or a difference in language implies a development or difference in thought. If the being or spirit worshipped has come to be designated by a proper name, he has lost much of the vagueness that characterises a nameless spirit, and he has come to be much more definite and much more personal.

Indeed, a change much more sinister, from the religious point of view, is wrought, when the transition from polydaemonism to polytheism is accomplished.

In the stage of human evolution known as animism, everything which acts—or is supposed to act—is supposed to be, like man himself, a person. But though, in the animistic stage, all powers are conceived by man as being persons, they are not all conceived as having human form : they may be animals, and have animal forms ; or birds, and have bird-form ; they may be trees, clouds, streams, the wind, the earthquake or the fire. In some, or rather in all, of these, man has at some time found the being or the power, greater than man, of whom he has at all times been in quest, with the enquiry, addressed to each in turn, 'Art thou there?' The form of the question, the use of the personal pronoun, shows that he is seeking for a person. And students of the science of religion are generally agreed that man, throughout the history of religion, has been seeking for a power or being superior to man and greater than he. It is therefore a personal power and a personal being that man has been in search of, throughout his religious history. He has pushed his search in many directions—often simultaneously in different directions ; and, he has abandoned one line of enquiry after another, because he has found that it did not lead him whither he would be. Thus, as we have seen, he pushed forward, at the same time, in the direction of fetishism and of polytheism, or rather of polydaemonism; but fetishism failed to bring him satisfaction, or rather failed to satisfy the common consciousness, the consciousness of the community, because it proved on trial to subserve the wishes—the anti-social wishes—of the individual, and not the interests of the community. The beings or powers that man looked to find and which he supposed he found, whether as fetishes in this or that object, or as daemons in the sky, the fire or the wind, in beast or bird or tree, were taken to be personal beings and personal powers, bearing the same relation to that in which, or through which, they manifested themselves, as man bears to his body. They do not seem to have been conceived as being men, or the souls of men which manifested themselves in animals or trees. At the time when polydaemonism has, as yet, not become polytheism, the personal beings, worshipped in this or that external form, have not as yet been anthropomorphised. Indeed, the process which constitutes the change from polydaemonism to polytheism consists in the process, or rather is the process, by which the spirits, the personal beings, worshipped in tree, or sky, or cloud, or wind, or fire came gradually to be anthropomorphised—to be invested with human parts and passions and to be addressed like human beings with proper names. But when anthropomorphic polytheism is thus pushed to its extreme logical conclusions, its tendency is to collapse in the same way, and for the same reasons, as fetishism, before it, had collapsed. What man had been in search of, from the beginning, and was still in search of, was some personal being or power, higher than and superior to man. What anthropomorphic polytheism presented him with, in the upshot, was with beings, not superior, but, in some or many cases, undeniably inferior to man. As such they could not thenceforth be worshipped. In Europe their worship was overthrown by Christianity. But, on reflection, it seems clear not only that, as such, they could not thenceforth be worshipped; but that, as such, they never had been worshipped. In the consciousness of the community, the object of worship had always been, from the beginning, some personal being superior to man. The apostle of Christianity might justifiably speak to polytheists of the God 'whom ye ignorantly worship.' It is true, and it is important to notice, that the sacrifices and the rites and ceremonies, which together made up the service of worship, had been consciously and intentionally rendered to deities represented in human form; and, in this sense, anthropomorphic deities had been worshipped. But, if worship is something other than sacrifice and rite and ceremony, then the object of worship—the personal being, greater than man—presented to the common consciousness, is something other than the anthropomorphic being, inferior in much to man, of whom poets speak in mythology and whom artists represent in bodily shape.

Just as fetishism developed and persisted, because it did contain, though it perverted, one element of religious truth—the accessibility of the power worshipped to the worshipper—so too anthropomorphism, notwithstanding the consequences to which, in mythology, it led, did contain, or rather, was based on, one element of truth, viz. that the divine is personal, as well as the human. Its error was to set up, as divine personalities, a number of reproductions or reflections of human personality. It leads to the conclusion, as a necessary consequence, that the divine personality is but a shadow of the human personality, enlarged and projected, so to speak, upon the clouds, but always betraying, in some way or other, the fact that it is but the shadow, magnified or distorted, of man. It excludes the possibility that the divine personality, present to the common consciousness as the object of worship, may be no reproduction of the human personality, but a reality to which the human personality has the power of approximating. Be this as it may, we are justified in saying, indeed we are compelled to recognise, that in mythology, all the world over, we see a process of reflection at work, by which the beings, originally apprehended as superior to man, come first to be anthropomorphised, that is to be apprehended as having the parts and passions of men, and then, consequently, to be seen to be no better than men. This discovery it is which in the long run proves fatal to anthropomorphism.

We have seen, above, the reason why fetishism becomes eventually distasteful to the common consciousness: the beings, superior to man, which are worshipped by the community, are worshipped as having the interests of the community in their charge, and as having the good of the community at heart; whereas a fetish is sought and found by the individual, to advance his private interests, even to the cost and loss of other individuals and of the community at large. Thus, from the earliest period at which beings, superior to man, are differentiated into gods and fetishes, gods are accepted by the common consciousness as beings who maintain the good of the community and punish those who infringe it; while fetishes become beings who assist individual members to infringe the customary morality of the tribe. Thus, from the first, the beings, of whom the community is conscious as superior to man, are beings, having in charge, first, the customary morality of the tribe; and, afterwards, the conscious morality of the community.

This conception, it was, of the gods, as guardians

of morality and of the common good, that condemned fetishism; and this conception it was, which was to prove eventually the condemnation of polytheism. A multitude of beings—even though they be divine beings—means a multitude, that is a diversity, of ideas. Diversity of ideas, difference of opinion, is what is implied by every mythology which tells of disputes and wars between the gods. Every god, who thus disputed and fought with other gods, must have felt that he had right on his side, or else have fought for the sake of fighting. Consequently the gods of polytheism are either destitute of morality, or divided in opinion as to what is right. In neither case, therefore, are the gods, of whom mythology tells, the beings, superior to man, who, from the beginning, were present in the common consciousness to be worshipped. From the outset, the object of the community's worship had been conceived as a moral power. If, then, the many gods of polytheism were either destitute or disregardful of morality, they could not be the moral power of which the common consciousness had been dimly aware: that moral power, that moral personality, must be other than they. As the moral consciousness of the community discriminated fetishes from gods and tended to rule out fetishes from the sphere of religion; so too, eventually, the moral consciousness of the community came to be offended by the incompatibility between the moral ideal and the conception of a multitude of gods at variance with each other. If the common consciousness was slow in coming to recognise the unity of the Godhead—and it was slower in some people than in others—the unity was logically implied, from the beginning, in the conception of a personal power, greater and higher than man, and having the good of the community at heart. The history of religion is, in effect, from one point of view, the story of the process by which this conception, however dim, blurred or vague, at first, tends to become clarified and self-consistent.

That, however, is not the only point of view from which the history of religion can, or ought to be, regarded. So long as we look at it from that point of view, we shall be in danger of seeing nothing in the history of religion but an intellectual process, and nothing in religion itself but a mental conception. There is, however, another element in religion, as is generally recognised; and that an emotional element, as is usually admitted. What however is the nature of that emotion, is a question on which there has always been diversity of opinion. The beings, who figured in the common consciousness as gods, were apprehended by the common consciousness as powers superior to man; and certainly as powers capable of inflicting suffering on the community. As such, then, they must have been approached with an emotion of the nature of reverence, awe or fear. The important, the determining, fact, however, is that they were approached. The emotion, therefore, which prompted the community to approach them, is at any rate distinguishable from the mere fright which would have kept the community as far away from these powers as possible. The emotion which prompted approach could not have been fear, pure and simple. It must have been more in the nature of awe or reverence; both of which feelings are clearly distinguishable from fear. Thus, we may fear disease or disgrace; but the fear we feel carries with it neither awe nor reverence. Again, awe is an inhibitive feeling, it is a feeling which—as in the case of the awe-struck person—rather prevents than promotes action or movement. And the determining fact about the religious emotion is that it was the emotion with which the community approached its gods. That emotion is now, and probably always was, reverential in character. The occasion, on which a community approaches its gods, often is, and doubtless often was, a time when misfortune had befallen the community. The misfortune was viewed as a visitation of the god's wrath upon his community; and fear—that 'fear of the Lord, which is the beginning of wisdom'—doubtless played a large part in the complex emotion which stirred the community, not to run away but to approach the god for the purpose of appeasing his wrath. In the complexity of an emotion which led to action of this kind, we must recognise not merely fear but some trust and confidence—so much, at least, as prevented the person who experienced it from running away simply. The emotion is not too complex for man, in however primitive a stage of development: it is not more complex than that which brings a dog to his master, though it knows it is going to be thrashed.

That some trust and confidence is indispensable in the complex feeling with which a community approaches its gods, for the purpose of appeasing their wrath—still more, for beseeching favours from them—seems indisputable. But we must not exaggerate it. Wherever there are gods at all, they are regarded by the community as beings who can be approached: so much confidence, at least, is placed in them by the community that believes in them. Even if they are offended and wrathful, the community is confident that they can be appeased: the community places so much trust in them. Indeed its trust goes even further: it is sure that they do not take offence without reasonable grounds. If they display wrath against the community and send calamity upon it, it is, and in the opinion of the community, can only be, because some member of the community has done that which he should not have done. The gods may be, on occasion, wrathful;

but they are just. They are from the beginning moral beings—according to such standard of morality as the community possesses—and it is breaches of the tribe's customary morality that their wrath is directed against. They are, from the beginning, and for long afterwards in the history of religion, strict to mark what is amiss, and, in that sense, they are jealous gods. And this aspect of the Godhead it is which fills the larger part of the field of religious consciousness, not only in the case of peoples who have failed to recognise the unity of the Godhead, but even in the case of a people like the Jews, who did recognise it. The other aspect of the Godhead, as the God, not merely of mercy and forgiveness, but of love, was an aspect fully revealed in Christianity alone, of all the religions in the world.

But the love God displays to all his children, to the prodigal son as well as to others, is not a mere attribute assigned to Him. It is not a mere quality with which one religion may invest Him, and of which another religion, with equal right, may divest Him. The idea of God does not consist merely of attributes and qualities, so that, if you strip off all the attributes and qualities, nothing is left, and the idea is shown to be without content, meaning or reality.

The Godhead has been, in the common consciousness, from the beginning, a being, a personal being, greater than man; and it is as such that He has manifested Himself in the common consciousness, from the beginning until the present day. To this personality, as to others, attributes and qualities may be falsely ascribed, which are inconsistent with one another and are none of His. Some of the attributes thus falsely ascribed may be discovered, in the course of the history of religion, to have been falsely ascribed; and they will then be set aside. Thus, fetishism ascribed, or sought to ascribe, to the Godhead, the quality of willingness to promote even the anti-social desires of the owner of the fetish. And fetishism exfoliated, or peeled off from the religious organism. Anthropomorphism, which ascribed to the divine personality the parts and passions of man, along with a power greater than man's to violate morality, is gradually dropped, as its inconsistency with the idea of God comes gradually to be recognised and loathed. So too with polytheism: a pantheon which is divided against itself cannot stand. Thus, fetishism, anthropomorphism and polytheism ascribe qualities to the Godhead, which are shown to be attributes assigned to the Godhead and imposed upon it from without, for eventually they are found by experience to be incompatible with the idea of God as it is revealed in the common consciousness.

On the other hand, the process of the history of religion, the process of the manifestation or revelation of the Godhead, does not proceed solely by this negative method, or method of exclusion. If an attribute, such as that of human form, or of complicity in anti-social purposes, is ascribed, by anthropomorphism or fetishism, to the divine personality, and is eventually felt by the common consciousness to be incompatible with the idea of God, the result is not merely that the attribute in question drops off, and leaves the idea of the divine personality exactly where it was, and what it was, before the attribute had been foisted on it. The incompatibility of the quality, falsely ascribed or assigned, becomes—if, and when, it does become—manifest and intolerable, just in proportion as the idea of God, which has always been present, however vaguely and ill-defined, in the common consciousness, comes to manifest itself more definitely. The attribution, to the divine personality, of qualities, which are eventually found incompatible with it, may prove the occasion of the more precise and definite manifestation; we may say that action implies reaction, and so false ideas provoke true ones, but the false ideas do not create the new ones. The false ideas may stimulate closer attention to the actual facts of the common consciousness and thus may stimulate the formation of truer ideas about them, by leading to a concentration of attention upon the actual facts. But it is from this closer attention, this concentration of attention, that the newer and truer knowledge comes, and not from the false ideas. What we speak of, from one point of view, as closer attention to the facts of the common consciousness, may, from another point of view, be spoken of as an increasing manifestation, or a clearer revelation, of the divine personality, revealed or manifested to the common consciousness. Those are two views, or two points of view, of one and the same process. But whichever view we take of it, the process does not proceed solely by the negative method of exclusion: it is a process which results in the unfolding and disclosure, not merely of what is in the common consciousness, at any given moment, but of what is implied in the divine personality revealed to the common consciousness. If we choose to speak of this unfolding or disclosure as evolution, the process, which the history of religion undertakes to set forth, will be the evolution of the idea of God. But, in that case, the process which we designate by the name of evolution, will be a process of disclosure and revelation. Disclosure implies that there is something to disclose; revelation, that there is something to be revealed to the common consciousness—the presence of the Godhead, of divine personality.

II

THE IDEA OF GOD IN MYTHOLOGY

THE idea of God is to be found, it will be generally admitted, not only in monotheistic religions, but in polytheistic religions also; and, as polytheisms have developed out of polydaemonism, that is to say, as the personal beings or powers of polydaemonism have, in course of time, come to possess proper names and a personal history, some idea of divine personality must be admitted to be present in polydaemonism as well as in polytheism; and, in the same way, some idea of a personality greater than human may be taken to lie at the back of both polydaemonism and fetishism.

If we wish to understand what ideas are in a man's mind, we may infer them from the words that he speaks and from the way in which he acts. The most natural and the most obvious course is to start from what he says. And that is the course which was followed by students of the history of religion, when they desired to ascertain what idea exactly man has had of his gods. They had recourse, for the information they wanted, to mythology. Later on, indeed, they proceeded to enquire into what man did, into the ritual which he observed in approaching his gods; and, in the next chapter, we will follow them in that enquiry. But in this chapter we have to ask what light mythology throws upon the idea man has had of his gods.

Before doing so, however, we cannot but notice that mythology and polytheism go together. Fetishism does not produce any mythology. Doubtless, the owner of a fetish which acts knows and can tell of the wonderful things it has done. But those anecdotes do not get taken up into the common stock of knowledge; nor are they handed down by the common consciousness to all succeeding generations of the community. Mythology, like language, is the work, and is a possession, of the common consciousness.

Polydaemonism, like fetishism, does not produce mythology; but, for a different reason. The beings worshipped in the period of polydaemonism are beings who have not yet come to possess personal names, and consequently cannot well have a personal history attached to them. The difficulty is not indeed an absolute impossibility. Tales can be told, and at a certain stage in the history of fiction, especially in the pre-historic stage, tales are told, in which the hero has no proper name: the period is 'once upon a time,' and the hero is 'a man' *simpliciter*. But myths are not told about 'a god' *simpliciter*. In mythology the hero of the myth is not 'a god,' in the sense of any god you like, but this particular, specified god. And the reason is clear. In fiction the artist creates the hero as well as the tale; and the primitive teller of tales did not find it always necessary to invent a name for the hero he created. The hero could, and did, get along for some time without any proper name. But with mythology the case is different. The personal being, superior to man, of whom the myth is told, is not the creation of the teller of the tale: he is a being known by the community to exist. He cannot therefore, when he is the hero of a myth, be described as 'a god—any god you like.' Nor is the myth a tale which could be told of any god whatever: if a myth is a tale, at any rate it is a tale which can be told of none other god but this. Indeed, a myth is not a tale: it is an incident—or string of incidents—in the personal history of a particular person, or being, superior to man.

It is then as polydaemonism passes into polytheism, as the beings of the one come to acquire personal names and personal history, and so to become the gods of the other, that mythology arises. It is under polytheism that mythology reaches its most luxuriant growth; and when polytheism disappears, mythology tends to disappear with it. Thus, the light which mythology may be expected to throw on the idea of God is one, which, however it may illumine the polytheistic idea of God, will not be found to shine far beyond the area of polytheism.

Myths then are narratives, in which the doings of some god or gods are related. And those gods existed in the belief of the community, before tales were told, or could be told, about them. Myths therefore are the outcome of reflection—of reflection about the gods and their relations to one another, or to men, or to the world. Mythology is not the source of man's belief of the gods. Man did not begin by telling tales about beings whom he knew to be the creations of his own imagination, and then gradually fall into the error of supposing them to be, after all, not creatures of his own imagination but real beings. Mythology is not even the source of man's belief in a plurality of gods: man found gods everywhere, in every external object or phenomenon, because he was looking for God everywhere, and to every object, in turn, he addressed the question, 'Art thou there?' Mythology was not the source of polytheism. Polytheism was the source of mythology. Myths preserve to us the reflections which men have made about their gods; and reflection, on any subject, cannot take place until the thing is there to be reflected upon. The result of prolonged reflection may be, indeed must be, to modify the ideas from which we started, for the better—or, it may be, for the worse. But, even so, the result of reflection is not to create the ideas from which it started.

From this point of view, it becomes impossible to accept the theory, put forward by Max Müller, that mythology is due to 'disease of language.' According to his theory, simple statements were made of such ordinary, natural processes as those of the rising, or the setting, of the sun. Then, by disease of language, the meaning of the words or epithets, by which the sun or the dawn were, at the beginning, designated or described, passed out of mind. The epithets then came to be regarded as proper names; and so the people, amongst which these simple statements were originally made, found itself eventually in possession of a number of tales told of persons possessing proper names and doing marvellous things. Thus, Max Müller's theory not only accounted for the origin of tales told about the gods: it also explained the origin of the gods, about whom the tales were told. It is a theory of the origin, not merely of mythology, but also of polytheism.

Thus, even on Max Müller's theory, mythology is the outcome of reflection—of reflection upon the doings and behaviour of the sun, the clouds, wind, fire etc. But, on his theory, the sun, moon etc., were not, at first, regarded as persons, at all: it was merely owing to 'disease of language' that they came to be so regarded. Only if we make this original assumption, can we accept the conclusions deduced from it; and no student now accepts the assumption: it is one which is forbidden by the well-established facts of animism. Sun, moon, wind and fire, everything that acts, or is supposed to act, is regarded by early man as animated by personal power. If, therefore, the external objects, to which man turned with his question, 'Art thou there?' were regarded by him, from the beginning, as animated by personal power, the theory that they were not so regarded falls to the ground; and, consequently, we cannot accept it as accounting for the origin of polytheism.

Doubtless, during the time of its vogue, Max Müller's theory was accepted precisely because it did profess to account for the origin of polytheism, and because it denied polytheism any religious value or meaning whatever. On the theory, polytheism did not originate from any religious sentiment whatever, but from a disease of language. And this was a view which naturally commended itself to those who were ready to say and believe that polytheism is not religion at all. But the consequences of saying this are such as to make any science of religion, or indeed any history of religion, impossible. Where the idea of God is to be found, there some religion exists; and to say that, in polytheism, no idea of God can be found, is out of the question. If then polytheism is a stage in the history of religious belief, we have to consider it in relation to the other stages of religious belief, which preceded or followed it. We have to relate the idea of God, as it appeared in polytheism, with the idea as it appeared in other stages of belief. In order to do this, we must first discover what the polytheistic idea of God is ; and for that purpose we must turn, at any rate at first, to the myths which embody the reflections of polytheists upon the attributes and actions of the Godhead, or of those beings, superior to man, whose existence was accepted by the common consciousness. It may be that the reflections upon the idea of God, which are embodied in mythology, have so tended to degrade the idea of God, that religious advance upon the lines of polytheism became impossible, just as the conception of God as a being who would promote the anti-social wishes of an individual, rendered religious advance upon the lines of fetishism impossible. In that case, religion would forsake the line of polytheism, as it had previously abandoned that of fetishism.

A certain presumption that myths tend to the degradation of religion is created by the mere use of the term 'mythology.' It has come to be a dyslogistic term, partly because all myths are lies, but still more because some of them are ignoble lies. It becomes necessary, therefore, to remind ourselves that, though we see them to be untrue, they were not regarded as untrue by those who believed in them; and that many of them were not ignoble. Aeschylus and Sophocles are witnesses, not to be disbelieved, on these points, In their writings we have the reflections of polytheists upon the actions and attributes of the gods. But the reflections made by Aeschylus and Sophocles, and their treatment of the myths, must be distinguished from the myths, which they found to hand, just as the very different treatment and reflection, which the myths received from Euripides, must be distinguished from them. In both cases, the treatment, which the myths met with from the tragedians, is to be distinguished from the myths, as they were current among the community before and after the plays were performed. The writings of the tragedians show what might be made of the myths by great poets. They do not show what the myths were in the common consciousness that made them. And the history of mythology after the time of the three great tragedians makes it clear enough that even so noble a writer as Aeschylus could not impart to mythology any direction other than that determined for it by the conditions under which it originated, developed and ran its course.

Mythology is the work and the product of the common consciousness. The generation existing at any time receives it from preceding generations;

civilised generations from barbarous, and barbarous generations from their savage predecessors. If it grows in the process of transmission, and so reflects to some extent the changes which take place in the common consciousness, it changes but little in character. The common consciousness itself changes with exceeding slowness; it retains what it has received with a conservatism like that of children's minds; and, what it adds must, from the nature of the case, be modelled on that which it has received, and be of a piece with it. But, though the common consciousness changes but slowly, it does change: with the change from savagery to civilisation there goes moral development. Some of the myths, which are re-told from one generation to another, may be capable of becoming civilised and moralised in proportion as do those who tell them; but some are not. These latter are incidents in the personal history of the gods, which, if told at all, can only be told, as they had been told from the beginning, in all their repulsiveness. They survive, in virtue of the tenacity and conservatism of the common consciousness; and, as survivals, they testify to the moral development which has taken place in the very community which conserves them. By them the eye of modern science measures the development and the difference between the stage of society which originally produced them and the stage which begins to be troubled by them.

They are valuable for the purposes of modern science because they are evidence of the continuity with which the later stages have developed from the earlier; and, also, because they are the first outward indications of the discovery which was eventually to be made, of the difference between mythology and religion—a difference which existed from the beginning of mythology, and all through its growth, though it existed in the sphere of feeling long before it found expression for itself in words.

The course of history has shown, as a matter of fact, that these repulsive and disgusting myths could not be rooted out without uprooting the whole system of mythology. But the course of history has also shown that religion could continue to exist after the destruction of mythology, as it had done before its birth. But, of this the generations to whom myths had been transmitted and for whom mythology was the accepted belief, could not be aware. In their eyes the attempt to discredit some myths appeared to involve—as it did really involve—the overthrow of the whole system of mythology. If they thought—as they undoubtedly did think—that the destruction of mythology was the same thing as the destruction of religion, their error was one of a class of errors into which the human mind is at no time exempt from falling. And they had this further excuse, that the destruction of mythology did logically and necessarily imply the destruction of polytheism. Polytheism and mythology were complementary parts of their idea of the Godhead. Demonstrations therefore of the inconsistency and immorality involved in their idea were purely negative and destructive; and they were, accordingly, unavailing until a higher idea of the unity of the Godhead was forthcoming.

Until that time, polytheism and mythology struggled on. They were burdened, and, as time went on, they were overburdened, with the weight of the repulsive myths which could not be denied and disowned, but could only be thrust out of sight as far, and as long, as possible. These myths, however offensive they became in the long run to the conscience of the community, were, in their origin, narratives which were not offensive to the common consciousness, for the simple reason that they were the work of the common consciousness, approved by it and transmitted for ages under the seal of its approval. If they were not offensive to the common consciousness at the time when they originated, and only became so later, the reason is that the morality of the community was less developed at the time of their origin than it came to be subsequently. If they became offensive, it was because the morality of the community tended to advance, while they remained what they had always been.

It may, perhaps, be asked, why the morality of the community should tend to change, and the myths of the community should not? The reason seems to be that myths are learned by the child in the nursery, and morality is learned by the man in the world. The family is a smaller community than the village community, the city, or the state; and the smaller the community, the more tenacious it is of its customs and traditions. The toys of Athenian children, which have been discovered, are, all, the toys which children continue to use to this day. In the Iliad children built sand-castles on the sea-shore as they do now; and the little child tugged at its mother's dress then as now. Children then as now would insist that the tales told to them should always be told exactly as they were first told. Of the discrepancy between the morality exhibited by the heroes of nursery-tales and that practised by the grown-up world the child has no knowledge, for the sufficient reason that he is not as yet one of the grown-up world. When he enters the grown-up world, he may learn the difference; but he can only enter the grown-up world, if there is one for him to enter; and, in the childhood of man, there is none which he can enter, for the adults themselves, though of larger growth, are children still in mind. Custom and tradition rule the adult community then as absolutely as they rule the child community. In course of time, the adult community may break the bonds of custom and tradition; but the community which consists of children treasures them and hands them on. Within the tribe, thenceforth, there are two communities, that of the adults and that of the children. The one community is as continuous with itself as the other; but the children's community is highly conservative of what it has received and of what it hands on—and that for the simple reason that children will be children still. It is this homogeneity of the children's community which enables it to preserve its customs, traditions and beliefs. And as long as the community of adults is homogeneous, it also departs but little from the customs, traditions and beliefs, which it has inherited from the same source as the children's community has inherited them. The two communities, the children's and the adults', originate and develop within the larger community of the tribe. They differentiate, at first, with exceeding slowness; the children's community changes more slowly even than the adults'—its weapons continue to be the bow and arrow, long after adults have discarded them; and the bull-roarer continues sacred in its eyes to a period when the adult community has not only discarded its use but forgotten its meaning. In its tales and myths it may preserve the memory of a stage of morality which the adult community has outgrown, and has left behind as far it has left behind the bull-roarer or the bow and arrow. And the stage of morality, of which it preserves the memory, is one from which the adult community in past time emerged. Having emerged, indeed, it found itself, eventually, when made to look back, compelled to condemn that which it looked back upon.

What, then, were these myths, with which the moralised community might find itself confronted? They were tales which originated in the mind of the community when it was yet immature. They preserve to us the reflections of the immature mind about the gods and what they did. And it is because the minds, which made these reflections, were immature, that the myths which embodied or expressed these reflections, were such as might be accepted by immature minds, but were eventually found intolerable by more mature minds. It may, perhaps, be said—and it may be said with justice—that the reflections even of the immature mind are not all, of necessity, erroneous, for it is from them that the whole of modern knowledge has been evolved or developed, just as the steam-plough may be traced back to the primitive digging-stick: reflection upon anything may lead to better knowledge of the thing, as well as to false notions about it. But the nations, which have outgrown mythology, have cast it aside because in the long run they became convinced that the notions it embodied were false notions. And they reached that conclusion on this point in the same way and for the same reason as they reached the same conclusion in other matters; for there is only one way. There is only one way and one test by which it is possible to determine whether the inferences we have drawn about a thing are true or false, and that is the test of experience. That alone can settle the question whether the thing actually does or does not act in the way, or display the qualities alleged. If it proves in our experience to act in the way, or to display the qualities, which our reflection led us to surmise, then our conception of the thing is both corrected and enlarged, that is to say, the thing proves to be both more and other than it was at first supposed to be. If experience shows that it is not what we surmised, does not act in the way or display the qualities our reflection led us to expect, then, as the conclusions we reached are wrong, our reflections were on a wrong line, and must have started from a false conception or an imperfect idea of the thing.

It is collision of this kind between the conclusions of mythology and the idea of the gods, as the guardians of morality, that rouses suspicion in a community, still polytheistic, first that the conclusions embodied in mythology are on a wrong line, and next that they must have started from a false conception or imperfect idea of the Godhead. By its fruits is the error found to be error—by the immorality which it ascribes to the very gods whose function it is to guard morality. Mythology is the process of reflection which leads to conclusions eventually discarded as false, demonstrably false to anyone who compared them with the idea of the Godhead which he had in his own soul. Mythology worked out the consequences of the assumption that it is to the external world we must look for the divine personality of whose presence in the common consciousness, the community has at all times, been, even though dimly, aware. Doubts as to the truth of myths were first aroused by the inconsistency between the myths told and the justice and morality which had been from the beginning the very essence of divine personality. The doubts arose in the minds and hearts of individual thinkers; and, if those individuals had been the only members of the community who conceived justice and morality to be essential qualities of the divine personality, then it would have been necessary for such thinkers first to convert the community to that view. Now, one of the consequences of the prevalence of mythology is that the community, amongst whom it flourishes, comes to be, if not doubtful, then at times forgetful, of the fact that the gods of the community are moral beings and the guardians of morality. That fact had to be dismissed from attention, for the time being, whenever certain myths were related. And, the more frequently a fact is dismissed from attention, the less likely it is to reappear on the surface of consciousness. Thus, the larger the part played by mythology in the field of the common consciousness, the greater its tendency to drive out from attention those moral qualities which were of the essence of divine personality. But, however large the part played by mythology, and however great its tendency to obliterate the moral qualities of the gods, it rarely, if indeed ever, entirely obliterates them from the field of the common consciousness. Consequently, the individual thinkers, who become painfully aware of the contrast and opposition between the morality, which is essential to a divine personality, and the immorality ascribed to the gods in some myths, have not to deal with a community which denies that the gods have any morality whatever, but with a community which is ready to admit the morality of the gods, whenever its attention is called thereto. Thus, though it may be that it is in this or that individual that the inconsistency between the moral qualities, which belong to the gods, and the immoral actions which mythology ascribes to the gods, first manifests itself, to his distress and disturbance, still what has happened in his case happens in the case of some, and may happen in the case of all, other members of the community. The inconsistency then comes to exist not merely for the individual but for the common consciousness.

It was the immorality of mythology which first drew the attention of believers in polytheism to the inconsistency between the goodness, which was felt to be of the essence of the divine nature, and the vileness, which was imputed to them in some myths; but it is the irrationality and absurdity of mythology that seems, to the modern mind, to be its most uniform characteristic. So long as the only mythology that was studied was the mythology of Indo-European peoples, it was assumed, without question, that the myths could not really be, or originally have been, irrational and absurd: they must conceal, under their seeming absurdity and outwardly irrational appearance, some truth. They must have had, originally, some esoteric meaning. They must have conveyed—allegorically, indeed—some profound truths, known or revealed to sages of old, which it was the business of modern students to re-discover in mythology. And accordingly profound truths—scientific, cosmographic, astronomical, geographical, philosophic or religious—were discovered. There was no knowledge which the early ancestors of the human race were not supposed to have possessed, and their descendants to have forgotten.

But, when it came to be discovered, and accepted,

that the ancestors of the Indo-European peoples had once been savages, and that savages, all the world over, possessed myths, it became impossible to maintain that such savages possessed in their mythologies treasures of truth either scientific or religious. Myths have no esoteric meaning. Obviously we must take them to be what we find them to be amongst present-day savages, that is, absurd and irrational stories, with no secret meaning behind them. Yet it is difficult, indeed impossible, to accept this as the last word on the subject. The stories are rejected by us, because they are patently absurd and irrational. But the savage does not reject them: he accepts them. And he could not accept and believe them, if he, as well as we, found them irrational and absurd. In a word, it is the same with the irrationality as it is with the immorality of mythology: myths are the work and the product of the common consciousness. As such, myths cannot be viewed as irrational by the common consciousness in which they originated, and by which they were accepted and transmitted, any more than they were regarded as immoral.

Obviously, the common consciousness which produces mythology cannot pronounce the myths, when it produces them, and accepts them, absurd. On the contrary, they are rational, in its eyes, and according to its level of understanding, however absurd the growth of knowledge may eventually show them to be. Myths, then, in their origin, are told and heard, narrated and accepted, as rational and intelligible. As narrated, they are narratives: can we say that they are anything more? or are they tales told simply for the pleasure of telling? Tales of this latter kind, pure fiction, are to be found wherever man is. But, we have already seen some points in which myths differ from tales of this kind: in fiction the artist creates his hero, but in myths the being superior to man, of whom the story is told is not the creation of the teller of the tale; he is a being known to the community to exist. Another point of difference is that a myth belongs to the god of whom it is told and cannot properly be told of any other god. These are two respects in which the imagination is limited, two points on which, in the case of myths, the creative imagination is, so to speak, nailed down. Is it subject to any further restriction in the case of myths? Granted that an adventure, when once it has been set down to one god, may not be set down to another, is the creative imagination free, in the case of mythology, as it is in the case of pure fiction, to invent the incidents and adventures, which eventually—in a lexicon of mythology—go to make up the biography of the god? The freedom, it appears, is of a strictly limited character.

It is an induction, as wide as the world—being based on mythologies from all parts of the world—that myths are aetiological, that their purpose is to give the reason of things, to explain the origin of fire, agriculture, civilisation, the world—of anything, in fact, that to the savage seems to require explanation. In the animistic period, man found gods everywhere because everywhere he was looking for gods. To every object that arrested his attention, in the external world, he put, or might put, the question, 'Art thou there?' Every happening that arrested the attention of a whole community, and provoked from the common consciousness the affirmation, 'Thou art there,' was, by that affirmation, accepted as the doing of a god. But neither at this stage, nor for long after, is there any myth. The being, whose presence is thus affirmed, has at first no name: his personality is of the faintest, his individuality, the vaguest. Mythology does not begin until the question is put, 'Why has the god done this thing?' A myth consists, or originally consisted, of the reason which was found and adopted by the common consciousness as the reason why the god did what he did do. It is in this sense that myths are aetiological. The imagination which produces them is, in a sense, a 'scientific imagination.' It works within limits. The data on which it works are that this thing was done, or is done, by this god; and the problem set to the mythological imagination is, 'Why did he, or does he, do it?' The stories which were invented to answer this question constituted mythology; and the fact that myths were invented for the purpose of answering this question distinguishes them from stories in the invention of which the imagination was not subject to restriction, was not tied down to this god and to this action of his, and was not limited to the sole task of imagining an answer to the question, 'Why did he do it?' All myths are narratives, but not all narratives are myths. Some narratives have men alone for their heroes. They are imaginative but not mythological. Some narratives are about gods and what they did. Their purpose is to explain why the gods did what they did do, and those narratives are mythological.

It may, perhaps, seem that the imagination of early man would from the first be set to work to invent myths in answer to the question, 'Why did the god do this thing?' But, as a matter of fact, man can get on for a long time without mythology. A striking instance of this is afforded by the *di indigites* of Italy. Over everything man did, or suffered, from his birth to his death, one of these gods or goddesses presided. The Deus Vagitanus opened the lips of the new-born infant when it uttered its first cry; the Dea Ossipago made the growing child's bones stout and strong; the Deus

Locutius made it speak clearly; the goddess Viriplaca restored harmony between husband and wife who had quarrelled; the Dea Orbona closed a man's eyes at death. These *di indigites* had shrines and received sacrifices. They were distinguished into gods and goddesses. Their names were proper names, though they are but words descriptive of the function which the deity performed or presided over. Yet though these *di indigites* are gods, personal gods, to whom prayer and sacrifice are offered, they have no mythology attached to them; no myths are told about them.

The fact thus forced on our notice by the *di indigites* of Rome should be enough to warn us that mythology does not of necessity spring up, as an immediate consequence of the worship of the gods. It may even suggest a reason why mythology must be a secondary, rather than a primary consequence of worship. The Romans were practical, and so are savages: if they asked the question, 'Why did this god do this thing?' they asked it in no spirit of speculation but for a practical, common-sense reason: because they did not want this thing done again. And they offered sacrifices to the god or goddess, with that end in view. The things with regard to which the savage community first asks the question, 'Why did the god do it?' are things disastrous to the community—plague or famine. The answer to the question is really implied by the terms in which the question is stated: the community, or some member of the community has transgressed; he must be discovered and punished. So long and so far as the question is thus put and thus answered, there is little room for mythology to grow in. And it did not grow round the *di indigites* in Italy, or round corresponding deities in other countries.

But the question, 'Why did the god do it?' is susceptible, on reflection, of another kind of answer. And from minds of a more reflective cast than the Roman, it received answer in the form of mythology, of aetiological myths. Mythology is the work of reflection: it is when the community has time and inclination to reflect upon its gods and their doings that mythology arises in the common consciousness. For everything which happens to him, early man has one explanation, if the thing is such as seems to him to require explanation, and the explanation is that this thing is the doing of some god. If the thing that arrests attention is some disaster, which calls for remedy, the community approaches the god with prayer and sacrifice; its object is practical, not speculative; and no myth arises. But if the thing that arrests attention is not one which calls for action, on the part of the community, but one which stimulates curiosity and provokes reflection, then the reflective answer to the question, why has this thing been done by whatever god that did it, is a myth.

Thus the mood, or state of mind, in which mythology originates is clearly different from that in which the community approaches its offended gods for the purpose of appeasing them. The purpose in the latter case is atonement and reconciliation. The state of mind in the former case is one of enquiry. The emotion, of mingled fear and hope, which constitutes the one state of mind, is clearly different from the spirit of enquiry which characterises and constitutes the other state of mind. The one mood is undeniably religious; the other, not so. In the one mood, the community feels itself to be in the presence of its gods; in the other it is reflecting and enquiring about them. In the one case the community appears before its god; in the other it is reflectively using its idea of god, for the purpose of explaining things that call for explanation. But the idea of God, when used in this way, for the purpose of explaining things by means of myths, is modified by the use it is put to. It is not merely that everything which happens is explained, if it requires explanation, as the doing of some god; but the motives which early man ascribed, in his mythological moments, to the gods—motives which only undeveloped man could have ascribed to them—became part of the idea of God on which mythology worked and with which myths had to do. The idea of god thus gradually developed in polytheistic myths, the accumulated reflections of savage, barbarous and semi-barbarous ancestors, tends eventually to provoke reaction. But why? Not merely because the myths are immoral and irrational. But because of the essential impiety of imputing immoral and irrational acts to the divine personality. Plainly, then, those thinkers and writers who were painfully impressed by such impiety, who were acutely conscious that divine personality was irreconcilable with immorality and irrationality, had some other idea of God than the mythological. We may go further: we may safely say that the average man would not have been perturbed, as he was, by Socrates, for instance, had he, also, not found within him some other idea of God than the mythological. And we can understand, to some extent, how this should be, if we call to mind that, though mythology grows and luxuriates, still the worship of the gods goes on. That is to say, the community, through it all, continues to approach its gods, for the purpose, and with the emotion of mingled fear and hope, with which it had always come into the presence of its gods. It is the irreconcilability of the mood of emotion, which is essentially religious, with the mythological mode of reflective thought, which is not, that tends to bring about the religious reaction against mythology. It is not however until the divergence between religion and mythology has become considerable that the irreconcilability becomes manifest. And it is in the experience of some individual, and not in the common consciousness, that this irreconcilability is first discovered. That discovery it is which makes the discoverer realise that it is not merely when he comes before the presence of his gods in their temples, but that, whenever his heart rises on the tide of mingled fear, hope and thanksgiving, he comes into the presence of his God. Having sought for the divine personality in all the external objects of the world around him in the end he learns, what was the truth from the beginning,—that it is in his heart he has access to his God.

The belief in gods does not of necessity result in a mythology. The instance of the *di indigites* of Italy is there to show that it is no inevitable result. But mythology, wherever it is found, is of itself sufficient proof that gods are, or have been, believed in ; it is the outcome of reflection and enquiry about the gods, whom the community approaches, with mingled feelings of hope and fear, and worships with sacrifice and prayer. Now, a mythology, or perhaps we should rather say fragments of a mythology, may continue to exist as survivals, long after belief in the gods, of whom the myths were originally told, has changed, or even passed away entirely. Such traces of gods dethroned are to be found in the folk-lore of most Christian peoples. Indeed, not only are traces of bygone mythology to be found in Christendom; but rites and customs, which once formed part of the worship of now forgotten gods; or it may be that only the names of the gods survive unrecognised, as in the names of the days of the week. The existence of such survivals in Europe is known; their history has been traced; their origin is undoubted. When, then, in other quarters of the globe than Europe, amongst peoples which are as old as any European people, though they have no recorded history, we find fragments of mythology, or of ritual, or mere names of gods, without the myths and the ritual which attach elsewhere to gods, the presumption is that here too we have to deal with survivals of a system of worship and mythology, which once existed, and has now gone to pieces, leaving but these pieces of wreckage behind. Thus, amongst the Australian black-fellows we find myths about gods who now receive no worship. But they never could have become gods unless they had been worshipped at some time; they could not have acquired the proper, personal names by which they are designated in these surviving myths, if they had not been worshipped long enough for the words which designate them to become proper names, i.e. names denoting no other person than the one designated by them.

Amongst other backward peoples of the earth we find the names of gods surviving, not only with no worship but no myths attached to them; and the inference plainly is that, as they are still remembered to be gods, they once were objects of worship certainly, and probably once were subjects of mythology. And if, of a bygone religious system all that remains is in one place some fragments of mythology, and in another nothing but the mere names of the gods, then it is nothing astonishing if elsewhere all that we find is some fragment of worship, some rite, which continues to be practised, for its own sake, even though all memory of the gods in whose worship it originated has disappeared from the common consciousness—a disappearance which would be the easier if the gods worshipped had acquired no names, or names as little personal as those of the *di indigites.* Ritual of this kind, not associated with the names of any gods, is found amongst the Australian tribes, and may be the wreckage of a system gone to pieces.

Here, too, there is opportunity again, for the same error as that into which students of mythology once fell before, when they found, or thought they found, in mythology, profound truths, known or revealed to sages of old. The survivals mentioned in the last paragraph may be interpreted as survivals of a prior monotheism or a primitive revelation. But if they are survivals, at all, then they are survivals from a period when the ancestors of the present-day Africans or Australian black-fellows were in an earlier stage of social development—in an earlier stage even of linguistic development and of the thought which develops with language—than their descendants are now. Even in that earlier stage of development, however, man sought for God. If he thought, mistakenly, to find Him in this or that external object, he was not wrong in the conviction that underlay his search—the conviction that God is at no time afar off from any one of us.

III

THE IDEA OF GOD IN WORSHIP

WE have found mythology of but little use in our search after the idea of God; and the reason, as we have suggested, is that myth-making is a reflective process, a process in which the mind reflects upon the idea, and therefore a process which cannot be set up unless the idea is already present, or, rather we should say, has already been presented. When it has been presented, it can become food for reflection, but not until then. If then we wish to discover where and when it is thus immediately presented, let us look for it in worship. If it is given primarily in the moment of worship, it may be reproduced in a secondary stage as a matter for reflection. Now, in worship—provided that it be experienced as a reality, and not performed as a conventionality—the community's purpose is to approach its God: let us come before the Lord and enter His courts with praise, are words which represent fairly the thought and feeling which, on ordinary occasions, the man who goes to worship—really—experiences, whether he be polytheist or monotheist. I have spoken of 'the moment of worship,' but worship is, of course, a habit: if it is not a habit, it ceases to be at all, in any effective sense. And it is a habit of the community, of the common consciousness, which is continuous through the ages, even though it slowly changes; and which, as continuous, is conservative and tenacious. Even when it has become monotheistic, it may continue to speak of the one God as 'a great god above all other gods,' in terms which are survivals of an earlier stage of belief. Such expressions are like the clouds which, though they are lifting, still linger round the mountain top: they are part of the vapour which had previously obscured from view the reality which was there, and cannot be shaken at any time.

Worship may include words spoken, hymns of praise and prayer; but it includes also things done, acts performed, ritual. It is these acts that are the facts from which we have now to start, in order to infer what we can from them as to the idea of God which prompted them. There is an infinite diversity in these facts of ritual, just as the gods of polytheism are infinite in number and kind. But if there is diversity, there is also unity. Greatly as the gods of polytheism differ from one another, they are at least beings worshipped—and worshipped by the community. Greatly as rituals vary in their detail, they are all ritual: all are worship, and, all, the worship rendered by the community to its gods. And there can be no doubt as to their object or the purpose with which the community practises them: that purpose is, at least, to bring the community into the presence of its Lord. We may safely say that there can be no worship unless there is a community worshipping and a being which is worshipped. Nor can there be any doubt as to the relation existing between the two. The community bow down and worship: that is the attitude of the congregation. Nor can there be any doubt as to the relation which the god bears, in the common consciousness, to his worshippers: he is bound to them by special ties—from him they expect the help which they have received in ages past. They have faith in him—else they would not worship him—faith that he will be what he has been in the past, a very help in time of trouble. The mere fact that they seek to come before him is a confession of the faith that is in them, the faith that they are in the presence of their God and have access to Him. However primitive, that is rudimentary, the worship may be; however low in the scale of development the worshippers may be; however dim their idea of God and however confused and contradictory the reflections they may make about Him, it is in that faith that they worship. So much is implied by worship—by the mere fact that the worshippers are gathered together for worship. If we are to find any clue which may give us uniform guidance through the infinite variety in the details of the innumerable rituals that are, or have been, followed in the world, we must look to find it in the purpose for which the worshippers gather together. But, if we wish to be guided by objective facts rather than by hasty, *a priori* assumptions, we must begin by consulting the facts: we must enquire whether the details of the different rituals present nothing but diversity, or whether there is any respect in which they show likeness or uniformity. There is one point in which they resemble one another; and, what is more, that point is the leading feature in all of them; they all centre round sacrifice. It is with sacrifice, or by means of sacrifice, that their gods are approached by all men, beginning even with the jungle-dwellers of Chota Nagpur, who sacrifice fowls and offer victims, for the purpose of conciliating the powers that send jungle-fever and murrain. The sacrificial rite is the occasion on which, and a means by which, the worshipper is brought into that closer relation with his god, which he would not seek, if he did not—for whatever reason—desire it. As bearing on the idea of

God, the spiritual import, and the practical importance, of the sacrificial rite is that he who partakes in it can only partake of it so far as he recognises that God is no private idea of his own, existing only in his notion, but is objectively real. The jungle-dweller of Chota Nagpur may have no name for the being to whom, at the appointed season and in the appointed place, he sacrifices fowls; but, as we have seen, the gods only come to have proper, personal names in slow course of time. He may be incapable of giving any account, comprehensible to the civilised enquirer, of the idea which he has of the being to whom he offers sacrifice: more accomplished theologians than he have failed to define God. But of the reality of the being whom he seeks to approach he has no doubt. It is not the case that the reality of that being, by whomsoever worshipped, is an assumption which must be made, or a hypothesis that must be postulated, for the sake of providing a logical justification of worship. The simple fact is that the religious consciousness is the consciousness of God as real, just as the common consciousness is the consciousness of things as real. To represent the reality of either as something that is not experienced but inferred is to say that we have no experience of reality, and therefore have no real grounds for inference. We find it preferable to hold that we have immediate consciousness of the real, to some extent, and that by inference we may be brought, to a larger extent, into immediate consciousness of the real.

Of the reality of Him, whom even the jungle-dweller of Chota Nagpur seeks to approach, it is only possible to doubt on grounds which seek to deny the ultimate validity of the common consciousness on any point. With the inferences which men have drawn about that reality, and the ideas those inferences have led to, the case is different. What exactly those ideas are, or have been, we have, more or less, to guess at, from such facts as the science of religion furnishes. One such set of facts is comprised under the term, worship; and of that set the leading fact everywhere is the rite of sacrifice. By means of it we may reasonably expect to penetrate to some of the ideas which the worshippers had of the gods whom they worshipped. Unfortunately, however, there is considerable difference of opinion, between students of the science of religion, as to the idea which underlies sacrifice.

One fact from which we may start is that it is with sacrifice that the community draws near to the god it wishes to approach. The outward, physical fact, the visible set of actions, is that the body of worshippers proceed, with their oblation, to the place in which the god manifests himself and is to be found. The inference which follows is that, corresponding to this series of outward actions, there is an internal conviction in the hearts and minds of the worshippers: they would not go to the place, unless they felt that, in so doing, they were drawing near to their god.

In thus drawing near, both physically and spiritually, they take with them something material. And this they would not do, unless taking the material thing expressed, in some way, their mental attitude, or rather their religious attitude. The attitude thus expressed must be part of, or implied by, the desire to approach the god both physically and spiritually. The fact that they carry with them some material thing, expresses in gesture-language—such as is used by explorers towards natives whose speech is unknown to them—the desire that actuates them. And thus much may be safely inferred, viz. that the desire is, at any rate, to prepossess favourably the person approached.

Thus man approaches, bearing with him something intended to please the god that he draws near. But though that is part of his intention, it is not the whole. His desire is that the god shall be pleased not merely with the offering but with him. What he brings—his oblation—is but a means to that end. Why he wishes the god to be pleased with him, we shall have to enquire hereafter. Thus far, however, we see that that is the wish and is the purpose intimated by the fact that he brings something material with him.

It seems clear also that the something material, with which the community draws near to its god, need only be something which is conceived to be pleasing to the god. All that is necessary is that it should express, or symbolise, the feeling with which the community draws near. So long as it does this, its function is discharged. What it is of importance to notice, and what is apt to be forgotten, is the feeling which underlies the outward act, and without which the action, the rite, would not be performed. The feeling is the desire of the worshipper to commend himself. If we take this point of view, then the distinction, which is sometimes drawn between offerings and sacrifice, need not mislead us. The distinction is that the term 'sacrifice' is to be used only of that which is consumed, or destroyed, in the service; while the term 'offering' is to be used only of what is not destroyed. And the reason for drawing, or seeking to draw, the distinction, seems to be that the destruction, or consumption, of the material thing, in the service, is required to prove that the offering is accepted. But, though this proof may have come, in some cases, to be expected, as showing that the community was right in believing that the offering would be acceptable; the fact remains that the worshippers would not start out with the offering in their hands, unless they thought, to begin with, that it was acceptable. They would not draw near to the god, with an offering about the acceptability of which they were in doubt. Anything therefore which they conceived to be acceptable would suffice to indicate their desire to please, and would serve to commend them. And the desire to do that which is pleasing to their god is there from the beginning, as the condition on which alone they can enter his presence. Neglect of this fact may lead us to limit unduly the potentialities contained in the rite of sacrifice, from the beginning.

The rite did, undoubtedly, in the long course of time, come in some communities to be regarded and practised in a spirit little better than commercial. Sacrifices came to be regarded as gifts, or presents, made to the god, on the understanding that *do ut des.* Commerce itself, when analysed, is nothing but the application of the principle of giving to get. All that is necessary, in order to reduce religion to commercial principles, is that the payment of vows made should be contingent on the delivery of the goods stipulated for; that the thing offered should be regarded as payment; that the god's favour should be considered capable of being bought. It is however in communities which have some aptitude for commerce and have developed it, that religion is thus interpreted and practised. If we go back to the period in the history of a race when commerce is as yet unknown, we reach a state of things when the possibility of thus commercialising worship was, as yet, undeveloped. At that early period, as in all periods, of the history of religion, the desire of the worshippers was to be pleasing, and to do that which was pleasing, to him whom they worshipped; and the offerings they took with them when they approached his presence were intended to be the outward and visible sign of their desire. But in some, or even in many, cases, they came eventually to rely on the sign or symbol rather than on the desire which it signified; and that is a danger which constantly dogs all ritual. Attention is concentrated rather on the rite than on the spiritual process, which underlies it, and of which the rite is but the expression; and then it becomes possible to give a false interpretation to the meaning of the rite.

In the case of the offerings, which are made in the earliest stages of the history of religion, the false interpretation, which comes in some cases to be put upon them by those who make the offerings, has been adopted by some students of the history of religion, as the true explanation, the real meaning and the original purpose of offerings and sacrifice. This theory —the Gift-theory of sacrifice—requires us to believe that religion could be commercialised before commerce was known; that religion consists, or originally consisted, not in doing that which is pleasing in the sight of God, but in bribing the gods; that the relatively late misinterpretation is the original and true meaning of the rite; in a word, that there was no religion in the earliest manifestation of religion. But it is precisely this last contention which is fatal to the Gift-theory. Not only is it a self-contradiction in terms, but it denies the very possibility of religious evolution. Evolution is a process and a continuous process: there is an unbroken continuity between the earliest and the latest of its stages. If there was no religion whatever in the earliest stages, neither can there be any in the latest. And that is why those who hold religion to be an absurdity are apt to adopt the Gift-theory: the Gift-theory implies a degrading absurdity from the beginning to the end of the evolutionary process—an unbroken continuity of absurdity. On the other hand, we may hold by the plain truth that there must have been religion in the earliest manifestations of religion, and that bribing a god is not, in our sense of the word, religious. In that case, we shall also hold that the offerings which have always been part of the earliest religious ritual were intended as the outward and visible sign or symbol of the community's desire to do that which was pleasing to their god; and that it is only in the course of time, and as the consequence of misinterpretation, that the offerings come to be regarded as gifts made for the purpose of bribing the gods or of purchasing what they have to bestow. Thus, just as, in the evolution of religion, fetishism was differentiated from polytheism, and was cast aside—where it was cast aside—as incompatible with the demands of the religious sentiment, so too the making of gifts to the gods, for the purpose of purchasing their favour, came to be differentiated from the service which God requires.

The endeavour to explain the history and purpose of sacrifice by means of the Gift-theory alone has the further disadvantage that it requires us to close our eyes to other features of the sacrificial rite, for, if we turn to them, we shall find it impossible to regard the Gift-theory as affording a complete and exhaustive account of all that there was in the rite from the beginning. Indeed, so important are these other features, that, as we have seen, some students would maintain that the only rite which can be properly termed sacrificial is one which presents these features. From this point of view, the term sacrifice can only be used of something that is consumed or destroyed in the service; while the term offering is restricted to things which are not destroyed. But, from this point of view, we must hold that sacrifices, to be sacrifices in the specific sense must not merely be destroyed or consumed, for then anything that could be destroyed by fire would be capable of becoming a burnt-offering; and the burning would simply prove that the offering was acceptable—a proof which may in some cases have been required to make assurance doubly sure, but which was really superfluous, inasmuch as no one who desires his offering to be accepted will make an offering which he thinks to be unacceptable. Sacrifices, to be sacrifices in the specific sense thus put upon the word, we must hold to be things which by their very nature are marked out to be consumed: they must be articles of food. But even with this qualification, sacrifices are not satisfactorily distinguished from offerings, for a food-offering is an offering, and discharges the function of a sacrifice, provided that it is offered. That it should actually be consumed is neither universally nor necessarily required. That it is often consumed in the service is a fact which brings us to a new and different feature of the sacrificial rite. Let us then consider it.

Thus far, looking at the rite on its outward side, from the point of view of the spectator, we have seen that the worshippers, carrying with them something material, draw near to the place where the god manifests himself. From this series of actions and gestures, we have inferred the belief of the worshippers to be that they are drawing near to their god both physically and spiritually. We have inferred that the material oblation is intended by the worshippers as the outward and visible sign of their wish to commend themselves to the god. We have now to notice what has been implied throughout, that the worshippers do not draw near to the god without a reason, or seek to commend themselves to him without a purpose. And if we consult the facts once more, we shall find that the occasions, on which the god is thus approached, are generally occasions of distress, experienced or apprehended. The feelings with which the community draws near are compounded of the fear, occasioned by the distress or danger, and the hope and confidence that it will be removed or averted by the step which they are taking. Part of their idea of the god is that he can and will remove the present, or avert the coming, calamity; otherwise they would not seek to approach him. But part also of their idea is that they have done something to provoke him, otherwise calamity would not have come upon them. Thus, when the worshippers seek to come into the presence of their god, they are seeking him with the feeling that he is estranged from them, and they approach him with something in their hands to symbolise their desire to please him, and to restore the relation which ordinarily subsists between a god and his worshippers. Having deposited the offering they bring, and having proffered the petition they came to make, they retire satisfied that all now is well. The rite is now in all its essential features complete. But though complete, as an organism in the early stages of its history may be complete, it has, like the organism, the power of growth; and it grows.

The conviction with which the community ends the rite is the joyful conviction that the trouble is over-past. The joy which the community feels often expresses itself in feast and song; and where the offerings are, as they most commonly are, food-offerings or animal-sacrifice, the feast may come to be regarded as one at which the god himself is present and of which he partakes along with his worshippers. The joy, which expresses itself in feast and song, may, however, not make itself felt until the prayer of the community has been fulfilled and the calamity has passed away; and then the feast comes to be of the nature of a joyful thank-offering. But it is probably only in one or other of these two cases that the offering comes to be consumed in the service of feast and song. And although the rite may and does grow in this way, still this development of it—'eating with the god'—is rather potentially than actually present in the earliest form of the rite.

From this point of view, sacrificial meals or feasts are not part of the ritual of approach: they belong to the termination of the ceremony. They mark the fact of reconciliation ; they are an expression of the conviction that friendly relations are restored. The sacrificial meal then is accordingly not a means by which reconciliation is effected, but the outward expression of the conviction that the end has been attained; and, as expressing, it has the force of confirming, the conviction. Where the sacrificial rite grows to comprehend a sacrificial feast or meal, there the food-offering or sacrifice is consumed in the service. But the rite does not always develop thus; and even without this development it discharges its proper function. Before this development, it is on occasions of distress that the god is approached by the community, in the conviction that the community has offended, and with the object of purging the community and removing the distress, of appeasing the god and restoring good relations. Yet even at this stage the object of the community is to be at one with its god—at-one-ment and communion so far are sought. There is implied the faith that he, the community's god, cannot possibly be for ever alienated and will not utterly forsake them, even though he be estranged for the time. Doubtless the feast, which in some cases came to crown the sacrificial rite, may, where it was practised amongst peoples who believed that persons partaking of common food became united by a common bond, have come to be regarded as constituting a fresh bond and a more intimate communion between the god and his worshippers who alike partook of the sacrificial meal. But this belief is probably far from being, or having been, universal; and it is unnecessary to assume that this belief must have existed, wherever we find the accomplishment of the sacrificial rite accompanied by rejoicing. The performance of the sacrificial rite is prompted by the desire to restore the normal relation between the community and its god. It is carried out in the conviction that the god is willing to return to the normal relation; when it has been performed, the community is relieved and rejoices, whether the rejoicing does or does not take form in a feast; and the essence of the rejoicing is the conviction that all now is well, a conviction which arises from the performance of the sacrificial rite and not from the meal which may or may not follow it.

Where the institution of the sacrificial feast did grow up, the natural tendency would be for it to become the most important feature in the whole rite. The original and the fundamental purpose of the rite was to reconcile the god and his worshippers and to make them at one: the feast, therefore, which marked the accomplishment of the very purpose of the rite, would come to be regarded as the object of the rite. In that, however, there is nothing more than the shifting forward of the centre of religious interest from the sacrifice to the feast: there is nothing in it to change the character or conception of the feast. Yet, in the case of some peoples, its character and conception did change in a remarkable way. In the case of some peoples, we find that the feast is not an occasion of 'eating with the god' but what has been crudely called 'eating the god.' This conception existed, as is generally agreed, beyond the possibility of doubt, in Mexico amongst the Aztecs, and perhaps—though not beyond the possibility of doubt—elsewhere.

The Aztecs were a barbarous or semi-civilised people, with a long history behind them. The circumstances under which the belief and practice in question existed and had grown up amongst them are clear enough. The Aztecs worshipped deities, and amongst those deities were plants and vegetables, such as maize. It was, of course, not any one individual specimen that they worshipped: it was the spirit, the maize-mother, who manifested herself in every maize-plant, but was not identical with any one. At the same time, though they worshipped the spirit, or species, they grew and cultivated the individual plants, as furnishing them with food. Thus they were in the position of eating as food the plant, the body, in which was manifested the spirit whom they worshipped. In this there was an outward resemblance to the Christian rite of communion, which could not fail to attract the attention of the

Spanish priests at the time of the conquest of Mexico, but which has probably been unconsciously magnified by them. They naturally interpreted the Aztec ceremony in terms of Christianity, and the spirit of the translation probably differs accordingly from the spirit of the original.

We have now to consider the new phase of the sacrificial—indeed, in this connection, we may say the sacramental—rite which was found in Mexico, and to indicate the manner in which it probably originated. The offerings earliest made to the gods were not necessarily, but were probably, food-offerings, animal or vegetable; and as we are not in a position to affirm that there was any restriction upon the kind of food offered, it seems advisable to assume that any kind of food might be offered to any kind of god. The intention of offerings seems to be to indicate merely that the worshippers desire to be pleasing in the sight of the god whom they wish to approach. At this, the simplest and earliest stage of the rite, the sacrificial feast has not yet come into existence: it is enough if the food is offered to the god; it is not necessary that it should be eaten, or that any portion of it should be eaten, by the community. There is evidence enough to warrant us in believing that generally there was an aversion to eating the god's portion. If the worshippers ate any portion, they certainly would not eat and did not eat, until after the god had done so. At this stage in the development of the rite, the offerings are occasional, and are not made at stated, recurring, seasons. The reason for believing this is that it is on occasions of alarm and distress that the community seeks to draw near its god. But though it is in alarm that the community draws nigh, it draws nigh in confidence that the god can be appeased and is willing to be appeased. It is part of the community's idea of its god that he has the power to punish; that he does not exercise his power without reason; and that, as he is powerful, so also he is just to his worshippers, and merciful.

But though occasional offerings, and sacrifices made in trouble to gods who are conceived to be a very help in time of trouble, continue to be made, until a relatively late period in the history of religion, we also find that there are recurring sacrifices, annually made. At these annual ceremonies, the offerings are food-offerings. Where the food-offerings are offerings of vegetable food, they are made at harvest time. They are made on the occasion of harvest; and that they should be so made is probably no accident or fortuitous coincidence. At the regularly recurring season of harvest, the community adheres to the custom, already formed, of not partaking of the food which it offers to its god, until a portion has been offered to the god. The custom, like other customs, tends to become obligatory : the worshippers, that is to say the community, may not eat, until the offering has been made and accepted. Then, indeed, the worshippers may eat, solemnly, in the presence of their god. The eating becomes a solemn feast of thanksgiving. The god, after whom they eat, and to whom they render thanks, becomes the god who gives them to eat. What is thus true of edible plants—whether wild or domesticated—may also hold true to some extent of animal life, where anything like a 'close time' comes to be observed.

As sacrificial ceremonies come to be, thus, annually recurring rites, a corresponding development takes place in the community's idea of its god. So long as the sacrificial ceremony was an irregularly recurring rite, the performance of which was prompted by the occurrence, or the threat, of disaster, so long it was the wrath of the god which filled the foreground, so to speak, of the religious consciousness; though behind it lay the conviction of his justice and his mercy. But when the ceremony becomes one of annual worship, a regularly recurring occasion on which the worshippers recognise that it is the god, to whom the first-fruits belong, who gives the worshippers the harvest, then the community's idea of its god is correspondingly developed. The occasion of the sacrificial rite is no longer one of alarm and distress; it is no longer the wrath of the god, but his goodness as the giver of good gifts, that tends to emerge in the fore-ground of the religious consciousness. Harvest rites tend to become feasts of thanksgiving and thank-offerings; and so, by contrast with these joyous festivals, the occasional sacrifices, which continue to be offered in times of distress, tend to assume, more and more, the character of sin-offerings or guilt-offerings.

We have, however, now to notice a consequence which ensues upon the community's custom of not eating until after the first-fruits have been offered to the god. Not only is a habit or custom hard to break, simply because it is a habit; but, when the habit is the habit of a whole community, the individual who presumes to violate it is visited by the disapproval and the condemnation of the whole community. When then the custom has established itself of abstaining from eating, until the first-fruits have been offered to the god, any violation of the custom is condemned by the community as a whole. The consequence of this is that the fruit or the animal tends to be regarded by the community as sacred to the god, and not to be meddled with until after the first-fruits have been offered to him. The plant or animal becomes sacred to the god because the community has offered it to him, and intends to offer it to him, and does offer it to him annually. Now it is not a necessary and inevitable consequence that an animal or plant, which has come to be sacred, should become divine. But where we find divine animals or animal gods—divine corn or corn-goddesses—we are entitled to consider this as one way in which they may have come to be regarded as divine, because sacred, and as deities, because divine. When we find the divine plant or animal constituting the sacrifice, and furnishing forth the sacrificial meal, there is a possibility that it was in this way and by this process that the plant or animal came to be, first, sacred, then divine, and finally the deity, to whom it was offered. In many cases, certainly, this last stage was never reached. And we may conjecture a reason why it was not reached. Whether it could be reached would depend largely on the degree of individuality, which the god, to whom the offering was made, had reached. A god who possesses a proper, personal name, must have a long history behind him, for a personal name is an epithet the meaning of which comes in course of time to be forgotten. If its meaning has come to be entirely forgotten, the god is thereby shown not only to have a long history behind him but to have acquired a high degree of individuality and personality, which will not be altered or modified by the offerings which are made to him. Where, however, the being or power worshipped is, as with the jungle-dwellers of

Chota Nagpur, still nameless, his personality and individuality must be of the vaguest; and, in that case, there is the probability that the plant or animal offered to him may become sacred to him; and, having become sacred, may become divine. The animal or plant may become that in which the nameless being manifests himself. The corn or maize is offered to the nameless deity; the deity is the being to whom the corn or maize is habitually offered; and then becomes the corn-deity or maize-deity, the mother of the maize or the corn-goddess.

Like the *di indigites* of Italy, these vegetation-goddesses are addressed by names which, though performing the function of personal names and enabling the worshippers to make appeals to the deities personally, are still of perfectly transparent meaning. Both present to us that stage in the evolution of a deity, in which as yet the meaning of his name still survives; in which his name has not yet become a fully personal name; and in which he has not yet attained to full personality and complete individuality. This want of complete individuality can hardly be dissociated from another fact which goes with it. That fact is that the deity is to be found in any plant of the species sacred to him, or in any animal of the species sacred to him, but is not supposed to be found only in the particular plant or animal which is offered on one particular occasion.

If the corn-goddess is present, or manifests herself, in one particular sheaf of corn, at her harvest festival this year, still she did manifest herself last year, and will manifest herself next year, in another. The deity, that is to say, is the species; and the species, and no individual specimen thereof, is the deity. That is the reason which prevents, or tends to prevent, deities of this kind from attaining complete individuality.

This want of complete individuality and of full personality it is which characterises totems. The totem, also, is a being who, if he manifests himself in this particular animal, which is slain, has also manifested himself and will manifest himself in other animals of the same species: but he is not identical with any particular individual specimen. Not only is the individuality of the totem thus incomplete, but in many instances the name of the species has not begun to change into a proper personal name for the totem, as 'Ceres' or 'Chicomecoatl' or 'Xilonen' have changed into proper names of personal deities. Whether we are or are not to regard the totem as a god, at any rate, viewed as a being in the process of acquiring individuality, he seems to be acquiring it in the same way, and by the same process, as corn-goddesses and maize-mothers acquired theirs, and to present to our eyes a stage of growth through which these vegetation-deities themselves have passed.

They also at one time had not yet acquired the personal names by which they afterwards came to be addressed. They were, though nameless, the beings present in any and every sheaf of corn or maize, though not cabined and confined to any one sheaf or any number of sheaves. And these beings have it in them to become—for they did become—deities. The process by which and the period at which they may have become deities we have already suggested: the period is the stage at which offerings, originally made at irregular times of distress, become annual offerings, made at the time of harvest; the process is the process by which what is customary becomes obligatory. The offerings at harvest time, from customary, become obligatory. That which is offered, is thereby sacred; the very intention to offer it, this year in the same way as it was offered last year, suffices to make it sacred, before it is offered. Thus, the whole species, whether plant or animal, becomes sacred, to the deity to whom it is offered: it is his. And if he be as vague and shadowy as the power or being to whom the jungle-dwellers of Chota Nagpur make their offerings at stated seasons, then he may be looked for and found in the plant or animal species which is his. The harvest is his alone, until the first-fruits are offered. He makes the plants to grow: if they fail, it is to him the community prays. If they thrive, it is because he is, though not identical with them, yet in a way present in them, and is not to be distinguished from the being who not only manifests himself in every individual plant or animal of the species, though not identical with any one, but is called by the name of the species.

Whether we are to see in totems, as they occur in Australia, beings in the stage through which vegetation deities presumably passed, before they became corn-goddesses and mothers of the maize, is a question, the answer to which depends upon our interpretation of the ceremonies in which they figure. It is difficult, at least, to dissociate those ceremonies from the ritual of first-fruits. The community may not eat of the animal or plant, at the appropriate season, until the head-man has solemnly and sparingly partaken of it. About the solemnity of the ceremonial and the reverence of those who perform it, there is no doubt. But, whereas in the ritual of first-fruits elsewhere, the first-fruits are, beyond possibility of doubt or mistake, offered to a god, a personal god, having a proper name, in Australia there is no satisfactory evidence to show that the offerings are supposed, by those who make them, to be made to any god; or that the totem-spirit, if it is distinguished from the totem-species, is regarded as a god. There has accordingly been a tendency on the part of students of the science of religion to deny to totemism any place in the evolution of religion, and even to regard the Australian black-fellows as exemplifying, within the region of our observation, a pre-religious period in the process of human evolution. This latter view may safely be dismissed as untenable, whether we do or do not believe totemism to have a religious side. There is sufficient mythology, still existing amongst the Australian tribes, to show that the belief in gods survives amongst them, even though, as seems to be the case, no worship now attaches to the gods, with personal names, who figure in the myths. That myths survive, when worship has ceased; and that the names of gods linger on, even when myths are no longer told of them, are features to be seen in the decay of religious systems, all the world over, and not in Australia alone. The fact that these features are to be found in Australia points to a consideration which hitherto has generally been overlooked, or not sufficiently weighed. It is that in Australia we are in the midst of general religious decay, and are not witnessing the birth of religion nor in the presence of a pre-religious period. From this point of view, the worship of the gods, who figure in the myths, has ceased, but their names live on. And from this point of view, the names of the beings worshipped, in the totemistic first-fruits ceremonies, have disappeared, though the ceremonies are elaborate, solemn, reverent, complicated and prolonged; and religion has been swallowed up in ritual.

Even amongst the Aztecs, who had reached a stage of social development, barbarous or semi-civilised, far beyond anything attained by the Australian tribes, the degree of personality and individuality reached by the vegetation deities was not such that those deities had strictly proper names: the deity of the maize was still only 'the maize-mother.' Amongst the Australians, who are so far below the level reached in Mexico, the beings worshipped at the first-fruits ceremonies may well have been as nameless as the beings worshipped by the jungle-dwellers of Chota Nagpur. Around these nameless beings, a ritual, simple in its origin, but luxuriant in its growth, has developed, overshadowing and obscuring them from our view, so that we, and perhaps the worshippers, cannot see the god for the ritual.

In Mexico the vegetation-goddesses struggled for existence amongst a crowd of more developed deities, just as in Italy the *di indigites* competed, at a disadvantage, with the great gods of the state. In Australia the greater gods of the myths seem to have given way before—or to—the spread of totemism. Where gods are worshipped for the benefits expected from them, beings who have in charge the food-supply of the community will be worshipped not only annually at the season of the first-fruits, but with greater zeal and more continuous devotion than can be displayed towards the older gods who are worshipped only at irregular periods. Not only does the existence of mythology in Australia indicate that the gods who figure in the myths were once worshipped, though worship now no longer is rendered to them; but the totemistic ceremonies by their very nature show that they are a later development of the sacrificial rite. The simplest form of the rite is that in which the community draw near to their god, bearing with them offerings, acceptable to the god: it is at a later stage in the development of the rite that the offerings, having been accepted by the god, are consumed by the community, as is the case with the totem animals and plants. At its earliest stage, again, the rite is performed, at irregular periods, on occasions of distress: it is only at a more advanced stage that the rite is performed at fixed, annual periods, as in Australia. And this change of periodicity is plainly connected with the growth of the conviction that the annual first-fruits belong to the gods—a conviction springing from the belief that they are annually accepted by the god, a belief which in its turn implies a prior belief that they are acceptable. In other words, the centre of religious interest at first lies in approaching the god, that is in the desire to restore the normal state of relations, which calamity shows to have been disturbed. But in the end, religious interest is concentrated on, and expressed by, the feast which terminates the ceremony and marks the fact that the reconciliation is effected. What is at first accepted by the god at the feast comes to be regarded as belonging to him and sacred to him: the worshippers may not touch it until a portion of it, the first-fruits, has been accepted by him. Thus the rite which indicates and marks his acceptance becomes more than ever the centre of religious interest. The rite may thus become of more importance than the god, as in Australia seems to be the case; for the performance of the rite is indispensable if the community is to be admitted to eat of the harvest. When this point of view has been reached, when the performance of the rite is the indispensable thing, the rite tends to be regarded as magical. If this is what has happened in the case of the Australian rite, it is but what tends to happen, wherever ritual flourishes at the expense of religion. If it were necessary to assume that only amongst the Australian black-fellows, and never elsewhere, did a rite, originally religious, tend to become magical, then it would be *a priori* unlikely, in the extreme, that this happened in Australia. But inasmuch as this tendency is innate in ritual, it is rather likely that in Australia the tendency has run its course, as it has done elsewhere, in India, for example, where, also, the sacrificial rite has become magical. Whether a rite, originally religious, will become assimilated to magic, depends very much on the extent to which the community believes in magic. The more the community believes in magic, the more ready it will be to put a magical interpretation on its religious rites. But the fact that, in the lower communities, religion is always in danger of sinking into magic, does not prove that religion springs from magic and is but one kind of magic. That view, once held by some students, is now generally abandoned. It amounts simply to saying once more that in the earliest manifestations of religion there was no religion, and that religion is now, what it was in the beginning—nothing but magic. If that position is abandoned, then religious rites are, in their very nature, and from their very origin, different from magical rites. Religious rites are, first, rites of approach, whereby the community draws nigh to its god; and, afterwards, rites of sacramental meals whereby the community celebrates its reconciliation and enjoys communion with its god. Those meals are typically cases of 'eating with the god,' celebrated on the occasion of first-fruits, and based on the conviction, which has slowly grown up, that 'the earth is the Lord's, and the fulness thereof.' Meals, such as were found in Mexico, and have left their traces in Australia, in which the fruit or the animal that was offered had come to be regarded as standing in the same relation to the god as an individual does to the species, are meals having the same origin as those in which the community eats with its god, but following a different line of evolution.

The object of the sacrificial rite is first to restore and then to maintain good relations between the community and its god. Pushed to its logical conclusion, or rather perhaps we should say, pushed back to the premisses required for its logical demonstration, the very idea of renewing or restoring relations implies an original understanding between the community and its god; and implies that it is the community's departure from this understanding which has involved it in the disaster, from which it desires to escape, and to secure escape from which, it approaches its god, with desire to renew and restore the normal relations. The idea that if intelligent beings do something customarily, they must do so because once they entered into a contract, compact or covenant to do so, is one which in Plato's time manifested itself in the theory of a social compact, to account for the existence of morality, and which in Japan was recorded in the tenth century A.D. as accounting for the fact that certain sacrifices were offered to the gods. Thus in the fourth ritual of 'the Way of the Gods'—that is Shinto—it is explained that the Spirits of the Storm took the Japanese to be their people, and the people of Japan took the Spirits of the Storm to be gods of theirs. In pursuance of that covenant, the spirits on their part undertook to be Gods of the Winds and to ripen and bless the harvest, while the people on their part undertook to found a temple to their new gods; and that is why the people are now worshipping them. It was, according to the account given in the fourth ritual, the gods themselves who dictated the conditions on which they were willing to take the Japanese to be their people, and fixed the terms of the covenant. So too in the account given in the sixth chapter of Exodus, it was Jehovah himself who dictated to Moses the terms of the covenant which he was willing to make with the children of Israel: 'I will take you to me for a people, and I will be to you a God.' In Japan it was to the Emperor, as high priest, that the terms of the covenant were dictated, in consequence of which the temple was built and the worship instituted.

The train of thought is quite clear and logically consistent. If the gods of the Winds were to be trusted—as they were unquestionably trusted—it must be because they had made a covenant with the people, and would be faithful to it, if the people were. The direct statement, in plain, intelligible words, in the fourth ritual, that a covenant of this kind had actually been entered into, was but a statement of what is implied by the very idea, and in the very act, of offering sacrifices. And sacrifices had of course been offered in Japan long before the tenth century: they were offered, and long had been offered annually to the gods of the Harvest. Probably they had been offered to the gods of the Storms long before they were offered to the gods of the Winds; and the procedure narrated in the fourth ritual records the transformation of the occasional and irregular sacrifices, made to the winds when they threatened the harvest with damage, into annual sacrifices, made every year as a matter of course. Thus, we have an example of the way in which the older sacrifices, made originally only in times of disaster, come to be assimilated to the more recent sacrifices, which from their nature and origin, are offered regularly every year. Not only is there a natural tendency in man to assimilate things which admit of assimilation and can be brought under one rule; but also it is advisable to avert calamity rather than to wait for it, and, when it has happened, to do something. It would therefore be desirable from this point of view to render regular worship to deities who can send disaster; and thus to induce them to abstain from sending it.

In the fourth Shinto ritual the gods of the Winds are represented as initiating the contract and prescribing its terms. But in the first ritual, which is concerned with the worship of the gods of the Harvest, it is the community which is represented as taking the first step, and as undertaking that, if the gods grant an abundant harvest, the people will, through their high priest, the Emperor, make a thank-offering, in the shape of first-fruits, to the gods of the Harvest. This is, of course, no more an historical account of the way in which the gods of the Harvest actually came to be worshipped, than is the account which the fourth Shinto ritual gives of the way the gods of the Winds came to be worshipped. In both cases the worship existed, and sacrifices had been made, as a matter of custom, long before any need was felt to explain the origin of the custom. As soon as the need was felt, the explanation was forthcoming: if the community had made these sacrifices, for as long back as the memory of man could run, and if the gods had granted good harvests in consequence, it must have been in consequence of an agreement entered into by both parties; and therefore a covenant had been established between them, on some past occasion, which soon became historical.

This history of the origin and meaning of sacrifice has an obvious affinity with the gift-theory of sacrifice. Both in the gift-theory and the covenant-theory, the terms of the transaction are that so much blessing shall be forthcoming for so much service, or so much sacrifice for so much blessing. The point of view is commercial; the obligation is legal; if the terms are strictly kept on the one part, then they are strictly binding on the other. The covenant-theory, like the gift-theory, is eventually discovered by spiritual experience, if pushed far enough, to be a false interpretation of the relations existing between god and man. Being an interpretation, it is an outcome of reflection—of reflection upon the fact that, in the time of trouble, man turns to his gods, and that, in returning to them, he escapes from his trouble. On that fact all systems of worship are based, from that fact all systems of worship start. If, as is the case, they start in different directions and diverge from one another, it is because men, in the process of reflecting upon that fact, come to put different interpretations upon it. And so far as they eventually come to feel that any interpretation is a misinterpretation, they do so because they find that it is not, as they had been taught to believe, a correct interpretation but a misinterpretation of the fact: there is found in the experience of returning to God, something with which the misinterpretation is irreconcilable; and, when the misinterpretation is dispersed, like a vapour, the vision of God, the idea of God, shines forth the more brightly. One such misinterpretation is the reflection that the favour of the gods can be bought by gifts. Another is the reflection that the gods sell their favours, on the terms of a covenant agreed upon between them and man. Another is that that which is offered is sacred, and that that which is sacred is divine—that the god is himself the offering which is made to him.

In all systems of worship man not only turns to his gods but does so in the conviction that he is returning, or trying to return, to them—trying to return to them, because they have been estranged, and access to them is therefore difficult. Accordingly, he draws near to them, bearing in his hands something intended to express his desire to return to them. The material, external symbol of his desire—the oblation, offering or sacrifice which he brings with him because it expresses his desire—is that on which at first his attention centres. And because his attention centres on it, the rite of sacrifice, the outward ceremony, develops in ways already described. The object of the rite is to procure access to the god; and the greater the extent to which attention is concentrated on the right way of performing the external acts and the outward ceremony, the less attention is bestowed upon the inward purpose which accompanies the outward actions, and for the sake of which those external actions are performed. As the object of the rite is to procure access, it seems to follow that the proper performance of the rite will ensure the access desired. The reason why access is sought, at all, is the belief—arising on occasions when calamity visits the community—that the god has been estranged, and the faith that he may yet become reconciled to his worshippers. The reason why his wrath descends, in the shape of calamities, upon the community, is that the community, in the person of one of its members, has offended the god, by breaking the custom of the community in some way. For this reason—in this belief and faith—access is sought, by means of the sacrificial rite; and the purpose of the rite is assumed to be realised by the performance of the ceremonies, in which the outward rite consists. The meaning and the value of the outward ceremonies consists in the desire for reconciliation which expresses itself in the acts performed; and the mere performance of the acts tends of itself to relieve the desire. That is why the covenant-theory of sacrifice gains acceptance: it represents—it is an official representation—that performance of the sacrificial ceremony is all that is required, by the terms of the agreement, to obtain reconciliation and to effect atonement. But the representation is found to be a misrepresentation: the desire for reconciliation and atonement is not to be satisfied by outward ceremonies, but by hearkening and obedience. 'To obey is better than sacrifice and to hearken than the fat of rams.' Sacrifice remains the outward rite, but it is pronounced to have value only so far as it is an expression of the spirit of obedience. Oblations are vain unless the person who offers them is changed in heart, unless there is an inward, spiritual process, of which the external ceremony is an expression. Though this was an interpretation of the meaning of the sacrificial rite which was incompatible with the covenant-theory and which was eventually fatal to it, it was at once a return to the original object of the rite and a disclosure of its meaning. Some such internal, spiritual process is implied by sacrifice from the beginning, for it is a plain impossibility to suppose that in the beginning it consisted of mere external actions which had absolutely no meaning whatever, for those who performed them; and it is equally impossible to maintain that such meaning as they had was not a religious meaning. The history of religion is the history of the process by which the import of that meaning rises to the surface of clear consciousness, and is gradually revealed. Beneath the ceremony and the outward rite there was always a moral and religious process—moral because it was the community of fellow-worshippers who offered the sacrifice, on occasions of a breach of the custom, that is of the customary morality, of the tribe; religious because it was to their god that they offered it. The very purpose with which the community offered it was to purge itself of the offence committed by one of its members. The condition precedent, on which alone sacrifice could be offered, was that the offence was repented of. From the beginning sacrifice implied repentance and was impossible without it. But it sufficed if the community repented and punished the transgressor: his repentance however was not necessary—all that was necessary was his punishment.

The re-interpretation of the sacrificial rite by the prophets of Israel was that until there was hearkening and obedience there could be nothing but an outward performance of the rite. The revelation made by Christ was that every man may take part in the supreme act of worship, if he has first become reconciled to his brother, if he has first repented his own offences, from love for God and his fellow-man. The old covenant made the favour of God conditional on the receipt of sacrificial offerings. The new covenant removes that limit, and all others, from God's love to his children: it is infinite love. It is not conditional or limited; conditional on man's loving God, or limited to those who love Him. Otherwise the new covenant would be of the same nature as the old. But love asks for love; the greater love for the greater love; infinite love for the greatest man is capable of. And it is hard for a man to resist love; impossible indeed in the end: all men come under and into the new covenant, in which there is infinite love on the one side, and love that may grow infinitely on the other. If it is to grow, however, it is in a new life that it must grow: a life of sacrifice, a life in which he who comes under the new covenant is himself the offering and the 'lively sacrifice.'

The worshipper's idea of God necessarily determines the spirit in which he worships. The idea of God as a God of love is different from the idea of Him as a God of justice, who justly requires hearkening and obedience. The idea of God as a God who demands obedience and is not to be put off with vain oblations is different from that of a God to whom, by the terms of a covenant, offerings are to be made in return for benefits received. But each and all of these ideas imply the existence, in the individual consciousness, and in the common consciousness, of the desire to draw near to God, and of the need of drawing nigh. Wherever that need and that desire are felt, there religion is; and the need and the desire are part of the common consciousness of mankind. From the beginning they have always expressed or symbolised themselves in outward acts or rites. The experience of the human race is testimony that rites are indispensable, in the same way and for the same reason that language is indispensable to thought. Thought would not develop were there no speech, whereby thought could be sharpened on thought. Nor has religion ever, anywhere, developed without rites. They, like language, are the work of the community, collectively; and they are a mode of expression which is, like language, intelligible to the community, because the community expresses itself in this way, and because each member of the community finds that other members have thoughts like his, and the same desire to draw near to a Being whose existence they doubt not, however vaguely they conceive Him, or however contradictorily they interpret His being. But, if language is indispensable to thought, and a means whereby we become conscious of each other's thought, language is not thought. Nor are rites, and outward acts, religion—indispensable though they be to it. They are an expression of it. They must be an inadequate expression; and they are always liable to misinterpretation, even by some of those who perform them. The history of religion contains the record of the misinterpretations of the rite of sacrifice. But it also records the progressive correction of those misinterpretations, and the process whereby the meaning implicit in the rite from the beginning has been made manifest in the end.

The need and the desire to draw nigh to the god of the community are felt in the earliest of ages on occasions when calamity befalls the community. The calamity is interpreted as sent by the god; and the god is conceived to have been provoked by an offence of which some member of the community had been guilty. We may say, therefore, that from the beginning there has been present in the common consciousness a sense of sin and the desire to make atonement. Psychologically it seems clear that at the present day, in the case of the individual, personal religion first manifests itself usually in the consciousness of sin. And what is true in the psychology of the individual may be expected within limits to hold true in the psychology of the common consciousness. But though we may say that, in the beginning, it was by the occurrence of public calamity that the community became conscious that sin had been committed, still it is also true to say that the community felt that it was by some one of its members, rather than by the community, that the offence had been committed, for which the community was responsible. It was the responsibility, rather than the offence, which was prominent in the common consciousness—as indeed tends to be the case with the individual also. But the fact that the offence had been committed, not by the community, but by some one member of the community, doubtless helped to give the community the confidence without which its attitude towards the offended power would have been simply one of fear. Had the feeling been one of fear, pure and unmixed, the movement of the community could not have been towards the offended being. But religion manifests itself from the beginning in the action of drawing near to the god. The fact that the offence was the deed of some one member, and not of the community as a whole, doubtless helped to give the community the confidence, without which its attitude towards the offended power would have been simply one of fear. But it also tended necessarily to make religion an affair of the community rather than a personal need : sin had indeed been committed, but not by those who drew near to the god for the purpose of making the atonement. They were not the offenders. The community admitted its responsibility, indeed, but it found one of its members guilty.

We may, therefore, fairly say that personal religion had at this time scarcely begun to emerge. And the reason why this was so is quite clear : it is that in the infancy of the race, as in the infancy of the individual, personal self-consciousness is as yet undeveloped. And it is only as personal self-consciousness develops that personal religion becomes possible. We must not however from this infer that personal religion is a necessary, or, at any rate, an immediate consequence of the development of self-consciousness. In ancient Greece one manifestation—and in the religious domain the first manifestation—of the individual's consciousness of himself was the growth of 'mysteries.' Individuals voluntarily entered these associations : they were not born into them as they were into the state and the state-worship. And they entered them for the sake of individual purification and in the hope of personal immortality. The desire for salvation, for individual salvation, is manifest. But it was in rites and ceremonies that the *mystae* put their trust, and in the fact that they were initiated that they found their confidence—so long as they could keep it. The traditional conviction of the efficacy of ritual was unshaken : and, so long as men believed in the efficacy of rites, the question, 'What shall I do to be saved?' admitted of no permanently satisfactory answer. The only answer that has been found permanently satisfying to the personal need of religion is one which goes beyond rites and ceremonies : it is that a man shall love his neighbour and his God.

But in thus becoming personal, religion involved man's fellow-men as much as himself. In becoming personal thus, religion became, thereby, more than ever before, the relation of the community to its God. The relation however is no longer that the community admits the transgressions of some one of its members: it prays for the forgiveness of 'our trespasses'; and though it prays for each of its members, still it is the community that prays and worships and comes before its God, as it has done from the beginning of the history of religion. It is with rites of worship that the community, at any period in the history of religion, draws nigh to its god; for its inward purpose cannot but reveal itself in some outward manifestation. Indeed it seeks to manifest itself as naturally and as necessarily as thought found expression for itself in the languages it has created ; and, though the re-action of forms of worship upon religion sometimes results, like the re-action of language upon thought, in misleading confusion, still, for the most part, language does serve to express more or less clearly—indeed we may say more and more clearly—that which we have it in us to utter.

As there are more forms of speech than one, so there are more forms of religion than one ; and as the language of savages who can count no higher than three is inadequate for the purposes of the higher mathematics, so the religion of man in the lower stages of his development is inadequate, compared with that of the higher stages. Nevertheless the civilised man can come to understand the savage's form of speech ; and it would be strange to say that the savage's form of speech, or that his form of religion, is unintelligible nonsense. Behind the varieties of speech and of religion there is that in the spirit of man which is seeking to express itself and which is intelligible to all, because it is in all. Though few of us understand any but civilised languages, we feel no difficulty in believing that savage languages not merely are intelligible but must have sprung from the same source as our own, though far inferior to it for every purpose that language is employed to subserve. The many different forms of religion are all attempts—successful in as many very various degrees as language itself—to give expression to the idea of God.

IV

THE IDEA OF GOD IN PRAYER

THE question may perhaps be raised, whether it is necessary for us to travel beyond worship, in order to discover what was, in early religions, or is now, the idea of God, as it presents itself to the worshipper. The answer to the question will depend partly on what we consider the essence of religion to be. If we take the view, which is held by some writers of authority on the history of religion, that the essence of religion is adoration, then indeed we neither need nor can travel further, for we shall hold that worship is adoration, and adoration, worship.

To exclude adoration, to say that adoration does not, or should not, form any part of worship, seems alike contrary to the very meaning of the word 'worship' and to be at variance with a large and important body of the facts recorded in the history of religion. The courts of a god are customarily entered with the praise which is the outward expression of the feeling of adoration with which the worshippers spiritually gaze upon the might and majesty of the god whom they approach. He is to them a great god, above all other gods. Even to polytheists, the god who is worshipped at the moment, is, at that moment, one than whom there is no one, and nought, greater, *quo nihil maius*. A god who should not be worshipped thus—a god who was not the object of adoration—would not be worthy of the name, and would hardly be called a god. So strongly is this felt that even writers who incline to regard religion as an illusion, define gods as beings conceived to be superior to man. The degree of respect, rising to adoration, will vary directly with the degree of superiority attributed to them; but not even in the case of a fetish, so long as it is worshipped, is the respect, which is the germ of adoration, wholly wanting. Even in the case of gods, on whom, on occasion, insult is put, it is precisely in moments when their superiority is in doubt that the worship of adoration is momentarily wanting. Worship without adoration is worship only in name, or rather is no worship at all. Only with adoration can worship begin: 'hallowed be Thy name' expresses the emotion with which all worship begins, even where the emotion has not yet found the words in which to express itself. It is because the emotion is there, pent up and seeking escape, that it can travel along the words, and make them something more than a succession of syllables and sounds.

If then it is on the wings of adoration that the soul has at all times striven to rise to heaven to find its God, even though it flutters but a little height and soon falls again to the ground, then we must admit that from the beginning there has been a mystical element, or a tendency to mysticism, in religion. In the lowest, and probably in the earliest, stages of the evolution of religion, this tendency is most manifest in individual members of the community, who are subject to 'possession,' ecstasy, trance and visions, and are believed, both by themselves and others, to be in especial communion with their god. This is the earliest manifestation of the fact that religion, besides being a social act and a matter in which the community is concerned, is also one which may profoundly affect the individual soul. But in these cases it is the exceptional soul which is alone affected—the seer of visions, the prophet. And it is not necessarily in connection with the ordinary worship, or customary sacrifice, that such instances of mystic communion with the gods are manifested. For the development of the mystical tendency of worship and sacrifice, we must look, not to the lowest, or to the earliest, stages of religious evolution, but to a later stage in the evolution of the sacrificial meal. It is where, as in ancient Mexico, the plant, or animal, which furnishes forth the sacrificial meal, is in some way regarded as, or identified with, the body of the deity worshipped, that the rite of sacrifice is tinged with mysticism and that all partakers of the meal, and not some exceptional individuals, are felt to be brought into some mystic communion with the god whom they adore.

In these cases, adoration is worship; and worship is adoration—and little more. Judging them by their fruits, we cannot say that the Mexican rites, or even the Greek mysteries, encourage us to believe that adoration is all that is required to make worship what the heart of man divines that it should be. Doubtless, this is due in part to the fact that the idea of God was so imperfectly disclosed to the polytheists of Mexico and Greece. Let us not therefore use Greece and Mexico as examples for the disparagement of mysticism or for the depreciation of man's tendency to seek communion with the Highest. Let us rather appeal at once to the reason which makes mysticism, of itself, inadequate to satisfy all the needs of man. The reason simply is that man is not merely a contemplative but an active being. If action were alien to his nature, then man might be satisfied to gaze, and merely gaze, on God. But man is active and not merely contemplative. We must therefore either hold that religion, being in its essence adoration and nothing more, has no function to perform, or sphere to fill, in the practical life of man; or else, if we hold that it does, or should, affect the practice of his life, we must admit that, though religion implies adoration always, it cannot properly be fulfilled in quietism, but must bear its fruit in what man does, or in the way he does it. The being or beings whom man worships are, indeed, the object of adoration, an object *quo nihil maius*; but they are something more. To them are addressed man's prayers.

It is vain to pretend that prayer, even the simple petition for our daily bread, is not religious. It may perhaps be argued that prayer is not essential to religion; that it has not always formed part of religion; and that it is incompatible with that acquiescence in the will of God, and that perfect adoration of God, which is religion in its purest and most perfect sense. Whether there is in fact any incompatibility between the petition for deliverance from evil, and the aspiration that God's will may be done on earth, is a question on which we need not enter here. But the statement that prayer has not always formed part of religion is one which it should be possible to bring to the test of fact.

In the literature of the science of religion, the prayers of the lower races of mankind have not been recorded to any great extent by those who have had the best opportunities of becoming acquainted with them, if and so far as they actually exist. This is probably due in part to their seeming too obvious and too trivial to deserve being put on record. It may possibly in some cases be due to the reticence the savage observes towards the white man, on matters too sacred to be revealed. The error of omission, so far as it can be remedied henceforth, will probably be repaired, now that savage beliefs are coming to be examined and recorded on the spot by scientific students in the interests of science. And the reticence of the savage promises to avail him but little: the comparative method has thrown a flood of light on his most sacred mysteries.

There may however be another reason why the prayers of the lower races have not been recorded to any great extent: they may not have been recorded for the simple reason that they may not have been uttered. The nature and the occasion of the rite with which the god is approached may be such as to make words superfluous: the purpose of the ceremony may find adequate expression in the acts performed, and may require no words to make it clear. If a community approaches its god with sacrifice or offering, in time of sore distress, it approaches him with full conviction that he understands the circumstances and the purpose of their coming. Words of dedication—'this to thee' is a formula actually in use—may be necessary, but nothing more. Indeed, the Australian tribes, in rites analogous to harvest-offerings, use no spoken words at all. We cannot, however, imagine that the rites are, or in their origin were, absolutely without meaning or purpose. We must interpret them on the analogy of similar rites elsewhere, the purpose of which is expressed not merely, as in Australia, by gesture-language, but is reinforced by the spoken word. Indeed, we may, perhaps, go even further, and believe that as gesture-language was earlier than speech, so the earliest rites were conducted wholly by means of ritual acts or gestures; and that it was only in course of time, and as a consequence of the development of language, that verbal formulae came to be used to give fuller expression to the emotions which prompted the rites.

If then we had merely to account for cases in which prayer does not happen to have been recorded as a constituent part of the rite of worship, we should not be warranted in inferring that prayer was really absent. The presumption would rather be that either the records are faulty, or that prayer, even though not uttered in word, yet played its part. The ground for the presumption is found in the nature of the occasions on which the gods are approached in the lower stages of religion. Those occasions are either exceptional or regularly recurring. The exceptional occasions are those on which the community is threatened, or afflicted, with calamity; and on such occasions, whether spoken words of prayer happen to have been recorded by our informants, or not, it is beyond doubt that the purpose of the community is to escape the calamity, and that the attitude of mind in which the god is approached is one of supplication or prayer. The regularly recurring occasions are those of seed-time and harvest, or first-fruits. The ceremonies at seed-time obviously admit of the presumption, even if there be no spoken prayers to prove it, that they too have a petitionary purpose; while the recorded instances of the prayers put up at harvest time, and on the occasion of the offering of first-fruits, suffice to show that thanksgiving is made along with prayers for continued prosperity.

It is however not merely on the ground of the absence of recorded prayers that it is maintained that there was a stage in the evolution of religion when prayer was unpractised and unknown. It is the presence and the use of spells which is supposed to show that there may have been a time when prayer was as yet unknown, and that the process of development was a progress from spell to prayer. On this theory, spells, in the course of time, and in accordance with their own law of growth, become prayers. The nature and operation of this law, it may be difficult or impossible now for us to observe. The process took place in the night of time and is therefore not open to our observation. But that the process, by which the one becomes the other, is a possible process, is perhaps shown by the fact that we can witness for ourselves prayer reverting or casting back to spell. Wherever prayers become 'vain repetitions,' it is obvious that they are conceived to act in the same way as the savage believes spells to act: the mere utterance of the formula has the same magical power, as making the sign of the cross, to avert supernatural danger. If prayers thus cast back to spells, it may reasonably be presumed that it is because prayer is in its origin but spell. It is because oxygen and hydrogen, combined, produce water, that water can be resolved into oxygen and hydrogen.

This theory, when examined, seems to imply that spell and prayer, so far from being different and incompatible things, are one and the same thing: seen from one point of view, and in one set of surroundings, it is spell; seen from another point of view, and in other surroundings, it is prayer. The point of view and the circumstances may change, but the thing itself remains the same always. What then is the thing itself, which, whether it presents itself as prayer or as spell, still always remains the same? It is, and can only be, desire. In spell and prayer alike the common, operative element present is desire. Desire may issue in spell or prayer; but were there no desires, there would be neither prayer nor spell.

That we may admit. But, then, we may, or rather must go further: if there were no desire, neither would there be any action, whatever, performed by man. Men's actions, however, differ endlessly from one another. They differ partly because men's desires, themselves, differ; and partly because the means they adopt to satisfy them differ also. It would be vain to say that different means cannot be adopted for attaining one and the same end. Equally vain would it be to say that the various means may not differ from one another, to the point of incompatibility. If then we regard prayer and spell as alike means which have been employed by man for the purpose of realising his desires, we are yet at liberty to maintain that prayer and spell are different and incompatible.

That there is a difference between prayer and spell—a difference at any rate great enough to allow the two words to be used in contradistinction to one another—is clear enough. The cardinal distinction between the two is also clear: a spell takes effect in virtue of the power resident in the formula itself or in the person who utters it; while a prayer is an appeal to a personal power, or to a power personal enough to be able to listen to the appeal, and to understand it, and to grant it, if so it seems good. That this difference obtains between prayer and spell will not be denied by any student of the science of religion. But if this difference is admitted, as admitted it must be, it is plain that prayer and spell are terms which apply to two different moods or states of mind. Desire is implied by each alike: were there no desire, there would be neither prayer nor spell. But, whereas prayer is an appeal to some one who has the power to grant one's desire, spell is the exercise of power which one possesses oneself, or has at one's command.

That the two moods are different, and are incompatible with one another, is clear upon the face of it: to beg for a thing as a mercy or a gift is quite different from commanding that the thing be done. The whole attitude of mind assumed in the one case is different from that assumed in the other. It is possible, indeed, to pass from the one attitude to the other. But it is impossible to say that the one attitude is the other. It is correct to say that the one attitude may follow the other. But it is to be misled by language to say that the one attitude becomes the other. It is possible for one and the same man to fluctuate between the two attitudes, to alternate between them—possible, though inconsistent. The child, or even that larger child, the man, may beg and scold, almost in the same breath. The savage, as is well known, will treat his fetish in the same inconsequential way. That it is inconsequential is a fact; but it is a fact which, if learned, is but very slowly learned. The process by which it is learned is part of the evolution of religion; and it is a process in the course of which the idea of God tends to disengage itself from the confusion of thought and the confusion of feeling, in which it is at first enshrouded.

We, indeed, at the present day, may see, or at any rate feel, the difference between magic and religion, between spell and prayer. And we may imagine that the difference, because real, has always been seen or felt, as we see and feel it. But, if we so imagine, we are mistaken. The difference was not felt so strongly, or seen so definitely, as to make it impossible to ascribe magic to Moses, or rain-making to Elijah. In still earlier ages, the difference was still more blurred. The two things were not discriminated as we now discriminate them: they were not felt then, as they are felt now to be inconsistent and incompatible. It was the likeness between the two that filled the field of mental vision, originally. Whether a man makes a petition or a command, the fact is that he wants something; and, with his attention centred on that fact, he may be but little aware, as the child is little, if at all, aware, that he passes, or is guilty of unreasonable inconsistency in passing, from the one mood to the other, and back again. It is in the course of time and as a consequence of mental growth that he becomes aware of the difference between the two moods.

If we insist on maintaining that, because spell and prayer are essentially different, men have at all times been fully conscious of the difference, we make it fundamentally impossible to explain the growth of religion, or to admit that it can have any growth. Just as, on the argument advanced in our first chapter, gods and fetishes have gradually been differentiated from some conception, prior to them, and indeterminate; just as magician and priest, eventually distinguished, were originally undistinguished, for a man of power was potentially both and might become either; so spell and prayer have come to be differentiated, to be recognised as different and fundamentally antagonistic, though originally the two categories were confused.

The theory that spell preceded prayer and became prayer, or that magic developed into religion, finds as little support in the facts afforded by the science of religion, as the converse theory of a primitive revelation and a paradisaical state in which religion alone was known. For what is found in one stage of evolution the capacity must have existed in earlier stages; and if both prayer and spell, both magic and religion, are found, the capacity for both must have pre-existed. And instead of seeking to deny either, in the interests of a pre-conceived theory, we must recognise both potentialities, in the interest of truth.

Just as man spoke, for countless thousands of

years, before he had any idea of the principles on which he spoke, of the laws of speech or of the grammar of his language; just as he reasoned, long before he made the reasoning process matter of reflection, and reduced it to the laws of logic; so from the beginning he was religious though he had no more idea that there were principles of religion, than that there were principles of grammar or laws of correct thought. 'First principles of every kind have their influence, and indeed operate largely and powerfully, long before they come to the surface of human thought and are articulately expounded' (Ferrier: *Institute of Metaphysics*, p. 13).

But this is not to say that primitive man argued, or thought, with never an error, or spoke with never a mistake, until by some catastrophe he was expelled from some paradise of grammarians and logicians. Though correct reasoning was logical before the time of Aristotle, and correct speech grammatical before the time of Dionysius Thrax; there was before, as there has been since, plenty both of bad logic and bad grammar. But that is very different from saying that, in the beginning, all reasoning was unsound, or all speech ungrammatical. To say so, would be as unmeaning and as absurd as to say that primitive man's every action was immoral, and his habitual state one of pure, unmitigated wickedness. If the assumption of a primitive paradise is unworkable, neither will the assumption of a primitive inferno act, whether it is for the evolution of the grammar of language or morality, or of logic or religion, that we wish to account. It is to ask too much, to ask us to believe that in the beginning there was only wrong-doing and no right, only error and no correctness of thought or speech, only spell and no prayer. And if both have been always, as they are now, present, there must also always have been a tendency in that which has prevailed to conquer. We may say that, in the process of evolution, man becomes aware of differences to which at first he gave but little attention; and, so far as he becomes conscious of them, he sets aside what is illogical, immoral, or irreligious, because he is satisfied it is illogical, immoral, or irreligious, and for no other reason.

The theory that spell preceded prayer in the evolution of religion proceeds upon a misconception of the process of evolution. At one time it was assumed and accepted without question that the vegetable and animal kingdoms, and all their various species, were successive stages of one process of evolution; and that the process proceeded on one line and one alone. On the analogy of the evolution of living beings, as thus understood, all that remained, when the theory of evolution came to be applied to the various forms of thought and feeling, was to arrange them also in one line; and that, it was assumed, would be the line which the evolution of religion had followed. On this assumption, either magic must be prior to religion, or religion prior to magic; and, on the principle that priority must be assigned to the less worthy, it followed that magic must have preceded religion.

It will scarcely be disputed that it was on the analogy of what was believed to be the course of evolution, in the case of vegetable and animal life, that the first attempts to frame a theory of the evolution of religion proceeded, with the result that gods were assumed to have been evolved out of fetishes, religion out of magic, and prayer out of spell. To disprove this, it is not necessary to reject the theory of evolution, or to maintain that evolution in religion proceeds on lines wholly different from those it follows elsewhere. All that is necessary is to understand the theory of the evolution of the forms of life, as that theory is held by naturalists now; and to understand the lines which the evolution of life is now held to have followed. The process of evolution is no longer held to have followed one line alone, or to have described but one single trajectory like that of a cannon-ball fired from a cannon. The process of evolution is, and has been from the beginning, dispersive. To borrow M. Bergson's simile, the process of evolution is not like that of a cannon-ball which followed one line, but like that of a shell, which burst into fragments the moment it was fired off; and these fragments being, as it were, themselves shells, in their turn burst into other fragments, themselves in their turn destined to burst, and so on throughout the whole process. The very lines, on which the process of evolution has moved, show the process to be dispersive. If we represent the line by which man has risen from the simplest forms of life or protoplasm by an upright line; and the line by which the lowest forms of life, such as some of the foraminifera, have continued on their low level, by a horizontal line starting from the bottom of the upright line, then we have two lines forming a right angle. One represents the line of man's evolution, the other that of the foraminifera. Between these two lines you may insert as many other lines as necessary. That line which is most nearly upright will represent the evolution of the highest form of vertebrate, except man; the next, the next highest; and so on till you come to the lines representing the invertebrates; and so on till you come to the lines which are getting nearer and nearer to the horizontal. Thus you will have a whole sheaf of lines, all radiating indeed from one common point, but all nevertheless dispersing in different directions.

The rush of life, the *élan de la vie*, is thus dispersive; and if we are to interpret the evolution of mental on the analogy of physical life, we shall find, M. Bergson says, nothing in the latter which compels us to assume either that intelligence is developed instinct, or that instinct is degraded intelligence. If that be so, then, we may say, neither is there anything to warrant us in assuming either that religion is developed magic, or magic degraded religion. Spell is not degraded prayer, nor is prayer a superior form of spell: neither does become or can become the other, though man may oscillate, with great rapidity, between the two, and for long may continue so to oscillate. The two moods were from the beginning different, though man for long did not clearly discriminate between the two. The dispersive force of evolution however tends to separate them more and more widely, until eventually oscillation ceases, if it does not become impossible.

The dispersive force of evolution manifests itself in the power of discrimination whereby man becomes aware of differences to which, in the first confusion of thought, he paid little attention; and ultimately may become conscious of the first principles of reason, morality or religion, as normative principles, in accordance with which he feels that he should act, though he has not always acted, and does not always act in accordance with them. In the beginning there is confusion of feeling and confusion of thought both as to the quarter to which prayer is addressed and as to the nature of the petitions which should be proffered. But we should be mistaken, if from the confusion we were to infer that there was no principle underlying the confusion. We should be mistaken, were we to say that prayer, if addressed to polytheistic gods, is not prayer; or that prayer, if addressed to a fetish, is not prayer. In both cases, the being to whom prayer is offered is misconceived and misrepresented by polytheism and fetishism; and the misconception is due to want of discrimination and spiritual insight. But failure to observe is no proof either that the power of observation is wanting or that there is nothing to be observed. The being to whom prayer is offered may be very different from the conception which the person praying has of him, and may yet be real.

Petitions, then, put up to polytheistic gods, or even to fetishes, may still be prayers. But petitions may be put up, not only to polytheistic gods, or to fetishes, but even to the one god of the monotheist, which never should be put up. 'Of thy goodness, slay mine enemies,' is, in form, prayer: it is a desire, a petition to a god, implying recognition of the superiority of the divine power, implying adoration even. But eventually it comes to be condemned as an impossible prayer: spiritually it is a contradiction in terms. If however we say that it is not, and never was, prayer; and that only by confusion of thought was it ever considered so, we may be told that, as a simple matter of actual fact, it is an actual prayer that was actually put up. That it ought not—from the point of view of a later stage in the development of religion—to have been put up, may be admitted; but that it was a prayer actually put up, cannot be denied. To this the reply seems to be that it is with prayer as it is with argument: a fallacy is a fallacy, just as much before it is detected as afterwards. The fact that it is not detected does not make it a sound argument; still less does it prove either that there are now no principles of correct reasoning or that there were none then; it only shows that there was, on this point, confusion of thought. So too we may admit—we have no choice but to admit—that there are spiritual fallacies, as well as fallacies of logic. Of such are the petitions which are in form prayers, just as logical fallacies are, in form, arguments. They may be addressed to the being worshipped, as fallacies are addressed to the reason; and eventually their fallacious nature may become evident even to the reason of man. But it is only by the evolution of prayer, that is by the disclosure of its true nature, that petitions of the kind in question come to be recognised and condemned as spiritual fallacies. The petitioner who puts up such petitions is indeed unconscious of his error, but he errs, for all that, just as the person who uses a fallacious argument may be himself the victim of his fallacy: but he errs none the less because he is deceived himself. There are normative principles of prayer as well as the normative principles of thought; and both operate 'long before they come to the surface of human thought and are articulately expounded.' It is in thinking that the normative principles of thought emerge. But it is by no means the case that they come to the surface of every man's thought. So too it is in prayer that the normative principles of prayer emerge; yet men require teaching how to pray. Some petitions are permissible, some not.

If then there are normative principles of prayer, just as there are of action, thought and speech; if there are petitions which are not permissible, and which are not and never can be prayers, though by a spiritual fallacy, analogous to logical fallacies, they may be thought to be prayers, what is it that decides the nature of an admissible petition? It seems to be the conception of the being to whom the petition is addressed. Thus it is that prayer throws light on the idea of God. From the prayers offered we can infer the nature of the idea. The confusion of admissible and inadmissible petitions points to confused apprehension of the idea of God. It is not merely imperfect apprehension but confused apprehension. In polytheism the confusion betrays itself, because it leads to collision with the principles of morality: of the gods who make war upon one another, each must be supposed to hold himself in the right; therefore either some gods do not know what is right, or there is no right to be known even by the gods. From this confusion the only mode of escape, which is satisfactory both to religion and to morality, is to recognise that the unity of morality and the unity of the godhead mutually imply one another. But so long as a plurality of gods, with a shifting standard of morality, is believed in, the distinction between admissible and inadmissible petitions cannot be firmly or correctly drawn.

A tribal god is petitioned to slay the tribe's enemies, because he is conceived as the god of the tribe and not the god of its enemies. If the declaration, that 'I am thy servant,' is affirmed with emphasis on the first personal pronoun, so as to imply that others are no servants of thine, the implication is that thy servants' enemies are thy enemies; whereas if there is, for all men, one God only, then all men are his servants, and not one person, or one tribe, alone. The conception of God as the god of one tribe alone is an imperfect and confused apprehension of the idea of God. But it is less so than is the conception of a god as belonging to one individual owner, as a fetish does. To a fetish the distinctive, though not the only, prayer offered, precisely is 'Slay mine enemies'; and therein it is that lies the difference between a fetish and a god of the community. The difference is the same in kind as that between a tribal god and the God of all mankind. The fetish and the tribal god are both inadequate ideas of God; and the inadequacy implies confusion—the confusion of conceiving that the god is there only to subserve the desires and to do the will of the individual worshipper or body of worshippers.

Escape from this confusion is to some extent secured by the fact that prayers to the community's god are offered by the community aloud, in public and as part of the public worship; and, consequently, with the object of securing the fulfilment of the desires of the community as a community. The blessing on the community is, at this stage, the only blessing in which the individual can properly share, and the only one for which he can pray to the god of the community. Thus the nature of the petitions, and the quarter to which permissible petitions can be addressed, are determined by the fact that prayer is an office undertaken by the community as a community. If the desires which an individual entertains are such as would be repudiated by the community, because injurious to the community, they cannot be preferred, in the presence of the community, to the god of the community; and thus permissible petitions begin to be differentiated from those which are impermissible—a normative principle of prayer emerges, and the idea of God begins to take more definite form, or to emerge somewhat from the mist which at first enveloped it.

But though permissible petitions be distinguished from petitions which are impermissible, it by no means follows that impermissible petitions cease to be put up. What actually happens is that since the community does not, and cannot, allow petitions, conceived to be injurious to itself, to be put up to its god, they are put up privately to a fetish; or, to put the matter more correctly, a being or power not identified with the welfare of the community is sought in such cases; and the being so found is known to the science of religion as a fetish. But though a fetish differs from a god, inasmuch as the fetish will, and a god will not, injure a member of the tribe, the distinction is not clear-cut. There are things which both alike may be prayed to do: both may be besought to do good to the individual who addresses them. To this protective mimicry the fetish owes in part its power of survival. For the same reason spell and magic contrive to continue their existence side by side with religion and prayer. What conduces to this result is that at first the god of the community is conceived as listening to the prayers of the community rather than of the individual: from the beginning it is part of the idea of God that He cares for all His worshippers alike. This conviction, to be carried out to its full consequences, both logical and spiritual, requires that each individual worshipper should forget himself, should renounce his particular inclinations, should abandon himself and long to do not his own will but that of God. But before self can be consciously abandoned, the consciousness of self must be realised. Before self-will can be surrendered, its existence must be realised. And self-consciousness, the recognition of the existence of the will and the reality of the self, comes relatively late both in the history of the community and in the personal history of the individual. At first the existence of the individual will and the individual self is not recognised by the community and is not provided for in the community's worship and prayers. It is the community, as a community, and not as so many individual worshippers, offering separate prayers, that first approaches the community's god. The existence of the individual worshipper, as an individual is not denied, it is simply unknown, or rather not realised by the community. But its stirrings are felt in the individual himself: he is conscious of desires which are other than those of the community, and the fulfilment of which forms no part of the community's prayers to the community's god. His self-consciousness, his consciousness of himself as contrasted with the community, is fostered by the growth of such desires. For the fulfilment of some of them, those which are manifestly anti-social, he must turn to his fetish, or rely upon the power of magic. Even for the fulfilment of those of his desires which are not felt to be anti-social, but which find no place in the prayers of the community, he must rely on some other power than that of the god of the community; and it is in spells, therefore, that he continues to trust for the fulfilment of these innocent desires, inasmuch as the prayers of the community do not include them.

The existence, in the individual, of desires, other than those of the community, wakes the individual to some consciousness of his individual existence. The effort to secure the fulfilment of those desires increases still further his self-consciousness, for he resorts to powers which are not exercised solely in the interests of the community, as are the powers of the community's god. But his increasing self-consciousness cannot and does not fail to modify his character and action as a worshipper of the community's gods. It modifies his relation to the community's gods in this sense, viz. that he appears before them not merely as a member of the community undistinguished from other members, but as an individual conscious to some extent of his individuality. He continues to take part in the worship of the gods, but he comes to it conscious of wishes of his own which may become petitions to the god, so far as they are not felt to be inconsistent with the good of the community.

Of this stage we have ample evidence afforded by the cuneiform inscriptions of Assyria. Spells employed to the hurt of any worshipper of the gods are spells against which the worshipper may properly appeal to the gods for protection. A god is essentially the protector of his worshippers, and he protects each as well as all of them. Each of them may therefore appeal to him for protection. But though any one of them may so appeal, it is apparently only in course of time that individual petitions of this kind come to be put up to the gods. And the evidence of the cuneiform inscriptions is particularly interesting and instructive on the way in which this came about.

In the 'Maklu' tablets we find that the writers of the tablets are, or anticipate that they may be, the victims of spells. The inscriptions themselves may be regarded, and by some authorities are described, as counter-charms or counter-spells. They do in fact include, though they cannot be said to consist of, counter-spells. Their typical feature is that they include some such phrase as, 'Whoever thou art, O witch, I bind thy hands behind thee,' or 'May the magic thou hast made recoil upon thyself.' If the victim is being turned yellow by sickness, the counter-spell is 'O witch, like the circlet of this seal, may thy face grow yellow and green.'

The ceremonies with which these counter-spells were performed are indicated by the words, and they are ceremonies of the same kind as those with which spells are performed: they are symbolic actions, that is to say, actions which express by gesture the same meaning and intention as are expressed by the words. Thus, from the words:

> 'As the water trickleth away from his body
> So may the pestilence in his body trickle away,'

it is obvious that this counter-spell accompanied a ceremonial rite of the kind indicated by the words. As an image of the person to be bewitched was used by the workers of magic, so an image of her 'who hath bewitched me' is used by the worker of the counter-spell, with the words:

> 'May her spell be wrecked, and upon her
> And upon her image may it recoil.'

If, now, such words, and the symbolical actions which are described and implied, were all that these Maklu tablets contained, it might be argued that these counter-spells were pure pieces of magic.

The argument would not indeed be conclusive, because though the sentences are in the optative mood, there would be nothing to show on what, or on whom, the speaker relied for the fulfilment of his wish. But as it happens, it is characteristic of these Maklu tablets that they are all addressed to the gods by name, e.g. 'May the great gods remove the spell from my body,' or 'O flaming Fire-god, mighty son of Anu! judge thou my case and grant me a decision! Burn up the sorcerers and sorceress!' It is the gods that are prayed to that the word of the sorceress 'shall turn back to her own mouth; may the gods of might smite her in her magic; may the magic which she has worked be crumbled like salt.'

Thus these Maklu petitions are not counter-spells, as at first sight they may appear; nor are they properly to be treated as being themselves spells for the purpose of counteracting magic. They are in form and in fact prayers to the gods 'to undo the spell' and 'to force back the words' of the witch into her own mouth. But though in the form in which these Maklu petitions are preserved to us, they appear as prayers to the gods, and not as spells, or counter-spells; it is true, and important to notice, that, in some cases, the sentences in the optative mood seem quite detachable from the invocation of the gods. Those sentences may apparently have stood, at one time, quite well by themselves, and apart from any invocation of the gods; that is to say, they may originally have been spells or counter-spells, and only subsequently have been incorporated into prayers addressed to the gods.

Let us then assume that this was the case with some of these Maklu petitions, and let us consider what is implied when we make the assumption. What is implied is that there are some wishes, for instance those embodied in these Maklu petitions, which may be realised by means of spells, or may quite appropriately be preferred to the gods of the community. Such are wishes for the well-being of the individual worshipper and for the defeat of evil-doers who would do or are doing him wrong. When it is recognised that individuals—as well as the community—may come with their plaints before the gods of the community, the functions of those gods become enlarged, for they are extended to include the protection of individual members of the community, as well as the protection of the community, as such; and the functions of the community's gods are thus extended and enlarged, because the members of the community have become, in some degree, individuals conscious of their individuality. The importance, for the science of religion, of this development of self-consciousness is that the consciousness of self must be realised before self can consciously be abandoned, that is before self-will can be consciously surrendered.

As is shown by the Maklu petitions, there may come, in the course of the evolution of religion, a stage in which it is recognised that the individual worshipper may petition the gods for deliverance from the evil which afflicts them. And the petitions used appear in some cases, as we have seen, to have been adopted into the ritual of the gods, word for word as they were found already in existence. If then they were, both in the words in which they were expressed, and in the purpose which they sought to achieve, such that they could be taken up, as they were and without change, into the ritual of the community's gods, it would seem that, even before they were so taken up, they could not have been wholly, if at all, alien to the spirit of religion. What marks them as religious, in the cuneiform inscriptions, is their context: it shows that the power, relied on for the accomplishment of the desires expressed in these petitions, was the power of the gods. Remove the context, and it becomes a matter of ambiguity, whether the wish is supposed, by those who utter it, to depend for its realisation on some power, possessed and exercised by those who express the wish, or whether it is supposed to depend on the good will of some being vaguely conceived, and not addressed by name. But if eventually the wish, and the words in which it was expressed, are taken up into the worship of the gods, there seems a balance of probability that the wish was from the beginning rather in the nature of religion than of magic, rather a petition than a command; though the categories were not at first discriminated, and there was at first no clear vision of the quarter from which fulfilment of the wish was hoped for.

From this point of view, optative sentences, sentences which express the wishes of him who pronounces them, may, in the beginning, well have been ambiguous, because there was, in the minds of those who uttered them, no clear conception of the quarter to which they were addressed: the idea of God may have been vague to the extreme of vagueness. Some of these optative sentences however, were such that the community as a whole could join in them; and they were potentially, and became actually, prayers to the god of the community. The being to whom the community, as a whole, could pray, was thereby displayed as the god of the community. The idea of God became, so far, somewhat less vague, somewhat more sharply defined. Optative sentences, however, in which the community could not join, in which no one but the person who framed them could take part, could not be addressed to the god of the community. The idea of God thus was defined negatively: there were wishes which could not be communicated to him—those which were repugnant to the well-being of the community.

The prayers of savages, that is of the men who are probably still nearest to the circumstances and condition of primitive man, furnish the material from which we can best infer what was the idea of God which was present in their consciousness at those moments when it was most vividly present to them. In view of the infinite number and variety of the forms of religion and religious belief, nothing would seem, *a priori*, more reasonable than to expect an equally infinite number of various and contradictory ideas. Especially should this seem a reasonable expectation to those who consider the idea of God to be fundamentally, and of its very nature, impossible and untenable. And so long as we look at the attempts which have been made, by means of reflection upon the idea, to body it forth, we have the evidence of all the mythologies to show the infinite variety of monstrosities, which reflection on the idea has been capable of producing. If then we stop there, our *a priori* expectation of savage and irrational inconsistency is fulfilled to abundance and to loathsome excess. But to stop there is to stop short, and to accept the speculations of the savage when he is reflecting on his experience, instead of pushing forward to discover for ourselves, if we may, what his experience actually was. To discover that, we cannot be content to pause for ever on his reflections. We must push back to the moment of his experience, that is to the moments when he is in the presence of his gods and is addressing them. Those are the moments in which he prays and in which he has no doubt that he is in communion with his gods. It is, then, from his prayers that we must seek to infer what idea he has of the gods to whom he prays.

When, however, we take his prayers as the evidence from which to infer his idea of God, instead of the luxuriant overgrowth of speculative mythology, we find everywhere a bare simplicity, and everywhere substantial identity. If this is contrary to our expectation and at first seems strange, let us bear in mind that the science of morals offers a parallel, in this respect, to the science of religion. At one time it was, unconsciously but none the less decidedly, assumed that savages had a multiplicity of irrational and disgusting customs but no morals. The idea that there could be a substantial identity between the moral rules of different savage races, and even between their moral rules and ours, was an idea that simply was not entertained. Nevertheless, it was a fact, though unnoticed; and now it is a fact which, thanks to Dr Westermarck, is placed beyond dispute. 'When,' he says, 'we examine the moral rules of uncivilised races we find that they in a very large measure resemble those prevalent among nations of culture.' The human spirit throughout the process of its evolution is, in truth, one; the underlying unity which manifests itself throughout the evolution of morality is to be found also in the evolution of religion; and it is from the prayers of man that we can infer it.

The first and fundamental article of belief implied by the offering of prayers is that the being to whom they are offered—however vaguely he may be conceived—is believed to be accessible to man. Man's cry can reach Him. Not only does it reach Him but, it is believed, He will listen to it; and it is of His very nature that He is disposed to listen favourably to it. But, though He will listen, it is only to prayers offered in the right spirit that He will listen. The earliest prayers offered are in all probability those which the community sends up in time of trouble; and they must be offered in the spirit of repentance. It is with the conviction that they have offended that the community first turns to the being worshipped, by whom they hope to be delivered from the evil which is upon them, and by whom they pray to be forgiven.

Next, the offering of prayer implies the belief that the being addressed, not merely understands the prayers offered, but has the power to grant them. As having not only the power, but also the will so to do, he is approached not only with fear but also with hope. No approach would or could be made, if nothing could be hoped from it; and nothing could be hoped, unless the being approached were believed to have the power to grant the prayer. The very fact that approach is made shows that the being is at the moment believed to be one with whom it rests to grant or refuse the supplication, one than whom no other is, in this respect at least, more powerful, *quo nihil maius.*

But prayers offered in time of trouble, though they be, or if they be, the earliest, are not the only prayers that are offered by early man. Man's wishes are not, and never were, limited: escape from calamity is not, and never has been, the only thing for which man is capable of wishing. It certainly is not the only thing for which he has been capable of praying. Even early man wishes for material blessings: the kindly fruits of the earth and his daily food are things for which he not only works but also prays. The negro on the Gold Coast prays for his daily rice and yams, the Zulu for cattle and for corn, the Samoan for abundant food, the Finno-Ugrian for rain to make his crops grow; the Peruvian prayed for health and prosperity. And when man has attained his wish, when his prayers have been granted, he does not always forget to render thanks to the god who listened to his prayer. 'Thank you, gods'; says the Basuto, 'give us bread to-morrow also.'

Whether the prayer be for food, or for deliverance from calamity, the natural tendency is for gratitude and thanks to follow, when the prayer has been fulfilled; and the mental attitude, or mood of feeling, is then no longer one of hope or fear, but of thankfulness and praise. It is in its essence, potentially and, to varying degrees, actually, the mood of veneration and adoration.

> 'My lips shall praise thee,
> So will I bless thee while I live:
> I will lift up my hands in thy name,
> And my mouth shall praise thee with joyful lips.'

From the prayers that are offered in early, if not primitive, religions we may draw with safety some conclusions as to the idea, which the worshippers had before their minds, of the being to whom they believed they had access in prayer. He was a being accessible in prayer; and he had it in his power, and, if properly approached, in his will, to deliver the community from material and external evils. The spirit in which he was to be properly approached was one of confession and repentance of offences committed against him: the calamities which fell upon the community were conceived to have fallen justly. He was not conceived to be offended without a cause. Doubtless the causes of offence, like the punishments with which they were visited, were external and visible, in the sense that they could be discovered and made plain to all who were concerned to recognise them. The offences were actions which not only provoked the wrath of the god, but were condemned by the community. They included offences which were purely formal and external; and, in the case of some peoples, the number of such offences probably increased rather than diminished as time went on. The *Surpu* tablets of the cuneiform inscriptions, which are directed towards the removal of the *mamit*, the ban or taboo, consequent upon such offences, are an example of this. Adultery, murder and theft are included amongst the offences, but the tablets include hundreds of other offences, which are purely ceremonial, and which probably took a long time to reach the luxuriant growth they have attained in the tablets. For ceremonial offences a ceremonial purification was felt to suffice. But there were others which, as the Babylonian Penitential Psalms testify, were felt to go deeper and to be sins, personal sins of the worshipper against his God. The penitent exclaims:

> 'Lord, my sins are many, great are my misdeeds.'

The spirit, in which he approaches his God, is expressed in the words:

> 'I thy servant, full of sighs, call upon thee.
> Like the doves do I moan, I am o'ercome with sighing,
> With lamentation and groaning my spirit is downcast.'

His prayer is that his trespasses may be forgiven:

> 'Rend my sins, like a garment!
> My God, my sins are unto seven times seven.
> Forgive my iniquities.'

And his hope is in God:

> 'Oh, Lord, thy servant, cast him not away,
> The sins which I have committed, transform by thy grace!'

The attitude of mind, the relation in which the worshipper finds himself to stand towards his God, is the same as that revealed in the Psalm of David:

> 'Wash me throughly from mine iniquity,
> And cleanse me from my sin.
> For I acknowledge my transgressions:
> And my sin is ever before me.
> Against thee, thee only, have I sinned.
> Cast me not away from thy presence.'

The earliest prayers offered by any community probably were, as we have already seen, those which were sent up in time of trouble and inspired by the conviction that the community's god had been justly offended. The psalms, from which quotations have just been given, show the same idea of God, conceived to have been justly offended by the transgressions of his servants. The difference between them is that, in the later prayers, the individual self-consciousness has come to realise that the individual as well as the community exists; that the individual, as well as the community, is guilty of trespasses; and that the individual, as well as the community, needs forgiveness. That is to say, the idea of God has taken more definite shape: God has been revealed to the individual worshipper to be 'My God'; the worshipper to be 'Thy servant'; and what is feared is not merely that the worshipper should be excluded from the community, but that he should be cast away from communion with God. The communion, aspired to, is however still such communion as may exist between a servant and his master.

Material and external blessings, further, are, together with deliverance from material and external evil, still the principal subjects of prayer in the Psalms both of the Old Testament and of the cuneiform inscriptions; and, so far as this is the case, the worshipper's prayer is that his individual will may be done, and it is because he has received material and external blessings, because his will has been done, that his joyful lips praise and bless the Lord. That is to say, the idea of God, implied by such prayer and praise, is that He is a being who may help man to the fulfilment of man's desires and to the realisation of man's will. The assumption required to justify this conception is that in man, man's will alone is operative, and never God's. This assumption has its analogy in the fact, already noticed, that in the beginning the individual is not self-conscious, or aware of the individuality of his own existence. When the individual's self-consciousness is thus but little, if at all, manifested, it is the community, as a community, which approaches its god and is felt to be responsible for the transgressions which have offended him. As self-consciousness comes to manifest itself, more and more, the sense of personal transgression and individual responsibility becomes more and more strong. If now we suppose that at this point the evolution, or unfolding, of the self ceases, and that the whole of its contents is now revealed, we shall hold that, in man, man's will alone can operate, and never God's. It is indeed at this point that non-Christian religions stop, if they get so far. The idea of God as a being whose will is to be done, and not man's, is a distinctively Christian idea.

The petition, which, as far as the science of religion enables us to judge, was the first petition made by man, was for deliverance from evil. The next, in historical order, was for forgiveness of sins; and, then, when society had come to be settled on an agricultural basis and dependent on the harvest, prayer was offered for daily bread. In the Lord's Prayer, the order of these petitions is exactly reversed. A fresh basis, or premiss, for them, is supplied. They are still petitions proper to put forward, if put forward in the consciousness of a fact, hitherto not revealed—that man may do not his own will but the will of Our Father, who is in heaven.

Prayer is thus, at the end, what it was at the beginning, the prayer of a community. But whereas at the beginning the community was the narrow and exclusive community of the family or tribe, at the end it is a community which may include all mankind. Thus, the idea of God has increased in its extension. In its intension, so to speak, it has deepened: God is disclosed not as the master and king of his subjects and servants, but as the Father in heaven of his children on earth. It has however not merely deepened, it has been transformed, or rather it is to be approached in a different mood, and therefore is revealed in a new aspect: whereas in the beginning the body of worshippers, whether it approached its god with prayer for deliverance from calamities or for material blessings, approached him in order that their desires might be fulfilled; in the end the worshipper is taught that approach is possible only on renunciation of his own desires and on acceptance of God's will. The centre of religion is transposed: it is no longer man and his desires round which religion is to revolve. The will of God is to be the centre, to which man is no longer to gravitate unconsciously but to which he is deliberately to determine himself. As in the solar system the force of gravity is but one, so in the spiritual system that which holds all spiritual beings together is the love which proceeds from God to his creatures and may increasingly proceed from them to Him. It is the substitution of the love of God for the desires of man which makes the new heaven and the new earth.

From the point of view of evolution the important fact is that this new aspect of the idea of God is not something merely superposed upon the old: if it were simply superposed, it would not be evolved. Neither is the disclosure, to the soul, of God as love, evolved from the conception of Him as the being from whom men may seek the fulfilment of their desires. To interpret the process of religious evolution in this way would be to misinterpret it, in exactly the same way as if we were to suppose that, only when the evolution of vegetable life had been carried out to the full in all its forms, did the evolution of animal life begin. Animals are not vegetables carried to a rather higher stage of evolution, any more than vegetables are animals which have relapsed to a lower stage. If then we are to apply the theory of evolution to spiritual life, as well as to bodily life, we must apply it in the same way. We must regard the various forms, in the one case as in the other, as following different lines, and tending in different directions from a common centre, rather than as different and successive sections of one and the same line. Spell no more becomes prayer than vegetables become animals. Impelled by the force of calamity to look in one direction—that of deliverance from pestilence or famine—early man saw, in the idea of God, a refuge in time of trouble. Moved at a later time by the feeling of gratitude, man found in the idea of God an object of veneration; and then interpreted his relation as that of a servant to his lord. Whichever way this interpretation was pushed—whether to mean that the servant was to do things pleasing to his lord, in order to gain the fulfilment of his own desires; or to imply that his transgressions stood ever between him and his offended master—further advance in that direction was impossible. A new direction, and therefore a fresh point of departure, was necessary. It was forthcoming in the Christian idea of God as the heavenly Father. That idea when revealed is seen to have been what was postulated but never attained by religion in its earlier stages. The petitions for our daily bread, for forgiveness of sins, and for delivery from evil, had as their basis, in pre-Christian religions, man's desire. In Christianity those petitions are preferred in the conviction that the making of them is in accordance with God's will and the granting of them in accordance with His love; and that conviction is a normative principle of prayer.

V

THE IDEA AND BEING OF GOD

MEN thought, spoke and acted for long ages before they began to reflect on the ways in which they did so; and, when they did begin to reflect, it was long before they discovered the principles on which they thought, spoke and acted, or recognised them as the principles on which man must speak, if he is to speak intelligibly; on which, as laws of thought, he must think, if he is to think correctly; and on which, as laws of morality, he must act, if he is to act as he should act.

But though many thousands of years elapsed before he recognised these laws, they were, all the time, the laws on which he had to think, speak and act, and did actually think, speak and act, so far as he did so correctly. When, then, we speak of the evolution of thought, speech and action, we cannot mean that the laws of thought, for instance, were in the beginning different from what they are now, and only gradually came to be what they are at present.

That would be just the same as saying that the law of gravitation did not operate in the way described by Newton until Newton formulated the law. The fact is that science has its evolution, just as thought, speech and action have. Man gradually and with much effort discovers laws of science, as he discovers the laws of thought, speech and action. In neither case does he make the laws; all that he does in either case is to come to recognise that they are there. But the recognition is a process, a slow process, attended by many mistakes and set-backs. And this slow process of the gradual recognition or discovery of fundamental laws, or first principles, is the process in which the evolution of science, as well as the evolution of thought, speech and action, consists. It is the process by which the laws that are at the bottom of man's thought, speech and action, and are fundamental to them, tend to rise to the surface of consciousness.

It is in this same process that the evolution of religion consists. It is the slow process, the gradual recognition, of the fundamental idea of religion—the idea of God—which tends to rise to the surface of the religious consciousness. Just as laws of thought, speech and action are implied by the very conception of right thought or speech or action, so the idea of God is implied by the mere conception of religion. It is implied always; it is implicit from the very beginning. It is disclosed gradually and imperfectly. The process of disclosure, which is the evolution of the idea, may, in many instances, be arrested at a stage of very early imperfection, by causes which make further development in that direction impossible; and then, if further progress is to be made, a fresh movement, in a fresh direction must be made. Just as men do not always think correctly, or act rightly, though they tend, in different degrees, to do so; so too, in religion, neither do they always move in the right direction, even if they move at all. They may even deteriorate, at times, in religion, as, at times, they deteriorate in morality. But it is not necessary to infer from this undoubted fact that there are no principles of either morality or religion. We are not led to deny the existence of the laws of logic or of grammar, because they are frequently disregarded by ourselves and others.

The principles, or rather some particular principle, of morality may be absolutely misconceived by a community, at some stage of its history, in such a way that actions of a certain kind are not condemned by it. The inconsistency of judgment and feeling, thus displayed, is not the less inconsistent because it is almost, if not entirely, unconscious. In the same way a community may fail to recognise a principle of religion, or may misinterpret the idea of God; still the fact that they misinterpret it is proof that they have it—if they had it not, they could not interpret it in different ways. And the different interpretations are the different ways in which its evolution is carried forward. Its evolution is not in one continuous line, but is radiative from one common centre, and is dispersive. That is the reason why the originators of religious movements, and the founders of religions, consider themselves to be restoring an old state of things, rather than initiating a new one; to be returning to the old religion, rather than starting a new religion. But in point of fact they are not reverting to a bygone stage in the history of religion; they are starting afresh from the fundamental principles of religion. From the central idea of religion, the idea of God, they move in a direction different from any hitherto followed. Monotheism may in order of time follow upon polytheism, but it is not polytheism under another name, any more than prayer is spell under another name. It is something very different: it is the negation of polytheism, not another form of it. It strikes at the roots of polytheism; and it does so because it goes back not to polytheism but to that from which polytheism springs, the idea of God; and starts from it in a direction which leads to a very different manifestation of the idea of God. And if monotheism displaces polytheism, it does so because it is found by experience to be the more faithful interpretation of that idea of God which even the polytheist has in his soul. In the same way, and for the same reasons, polytheism is not fetishism under another name. The gods of a community are not the fetishes of individuals. The difference between them is not a mere difference of name. Polytheism may, or may not, follow, in order of time, upon fetishism; but polytheism is not merely a form of fetishism. The two are different, and largely inconsistent, interpretations, or misinterpretations, of the same fundamental idea of God. They move in different directions, and are felt by the communities in which they are found, to tend in the direction of very different ends—the one to the good of the community, the other, in its most characteristic manifestations, to the injury of the community. In fetishism and polytheism we see the radiative, dispersive, force of evolution manifesting itself, just as in polytheism and monotheism. The different lines of evolution radiate in different directions, but those lines, all point to a common centre of dispersion—the idea of God. But fetishism, polytheism and monotheism are not different and successive stages of one line of evolution, following the same direction. They are lines of different lengths, moving in different directions, though springing from a common centre—the soul of man. It is because they have a common centre, that man, whichever line he has followed, can fall back upon it and start afresh.

The fact that men fall victims to logical fallacies does not shake our faith in the validity of the principles of reason; nor does the fact that false reasoning abounds the more, the lower we descend in the scale of humanity, lead us to believe that the principles of reason are invalid and non-existent there. Still less do we believe that, because immature minds reason often incorrectly, therefore correct reasoning is for all men an impossibility and a contradiction in terms. And these considerations apply in just the same way to the principles of religion and the idea of God, as to the principles of reason. Yet we are sometimes invited to believe that the existence of religious fallacies, or fallacious religions, is of itself enough to prove that there is no validity in the principles of religion, no reality in the idea of God; that because the uncultured races of mankind are the victims of error in religion, there is in religion no truth at all: the religion of civilised mankind consists but of the errors of the savage disguised in civilised garb. So far as this view is supposed to be the outcome of the study of the evolution of religion, it is due probably to the conception of evolution from which it proceeds. It proceeds on the assumption that the process of evolution exhibits the continuity of one and the same continuous line. It ignores the radiative, dispersive movement of evolution in different lines; and overlooks the fact that new forms of religion are all re-births, renaissances, and spring not from one another, but from the soul of man, in which is found the idea of God. It further assumes not merely that there are errors but that there is no truth whatever in the lowest, or the earliest, forms of religion; and that therefore neither is there any truth in the highest. But this assumption, if applied to the principles of thought, speech or action, would equally prove thought to be irrational, speech unintelligible, moral action absurd; and evolution would be the process by which this fundamental irrationality, unintelligibility and absurdity was worked out.

Either this is the conclusion, or some means must be sought whereby to distinguish the evolution of religion from the evolution of thought, speech and morals, and to show that—whereas in the case of the latter, evolution is the process in which the principles whereon man should think, speak and act, tend to manifest themselves with increasing clearness—in the case of religion, there is no such progressive revelation, and no first principle, or fundamental idea, which all forms of religion seek to express. But any attempt to show this is hopeless: the science of religion is engaged throughout in ascertaining and comparing the ideas which the various races of men have had of their gods; and in tracing the evolution of the idea of God.

The science of religion, however, it may be said, is concerned exclusively with the evolution, and not in the least with the value or validity, of the idea. But neither, we must remember, is it concerned to dispute its value or to deny its validity; and no man can help drawing his own conclusions from the established fact that the idea is to be found wherever man is to be found. If, however, by the idea of God we mean simply an intellectual idea, merely a verbal proposition, we shall be in danger of drawing erroneous conclusions. The historian of religion, in discussing the idea of God, its manifestations and its evolution, is bound to express himself in words, and to reduce what he has to say to a series of verbal propositions. Nothing, therefore, is more natural than to imagine that the idea of God is a verbal, intellectual proposition; and nothing is more misleading. If we start from this misleading notion, then, as words are but words, we may be led to imagine that the idea of God is nothing more or other than the words: it is mere words. If however this conclusion is, for any reason, displeasing to us, and if we stick to the premiss that the idea of God is a verbal proposition, then we shall naturally draw a distinction between the idea of God and the being of God; and, having thus fixed a great gulf between the idea and the being of God, we shall be faced with the difficulty of crossing it. We may then feel it to be not merely difficult but impossible to get logically to the other side of the gulf; that is to say, we shall conclude that the being of God is an inference, but an inference which never can be logically verified: the inference may be a correct or an incorrect inference, but we cannot possibly know which it is. From the idea of God we can never logically infer His being. Since then no logic will carry us over the chasm we have fixed between the idea and the being of God, if we are to cross it, we must jump it: we must take the leap of faith, we must believe the passage possible, just because it is impossible. And those who take the leap, do land safely—we have their own testimony to that—as safely as, in *King Lear*, Gloucester leaps from the cliff of Dover; and they well may

> 'Think that the clearest gods, who make them honours
> Of men's impossibilities, have preserv'd them.'

But, in Gloucester's case, there was no cliff and no abyss; and, in our case, it may be well to enquire whether the great gulf between the idea and the being of God has any more reality than that down which Gloucester, precipitating, flung himself. The premiss, that the idea of God is a mere verbal proposition, may be a premiss as imaginary as that from which Gloucester leaped. If the idea of God is merely a proposition in words, and if words are but words, then the gulf between idea and being is real. If the being of God is an inference from the idea of God, it is merely an inference, and an inference of no logical value. And the same remark holds equally true, if we apply it to the case of any finite personal being: if the being of our neighbours were an inference from the idea we have formed of them, it also would be an inference of no logical value. But, fortunately, their being does not depend on the idea we have formed of them: it partially reveals itself to us in our idea of them, and partially is obscured by it. It is a fact of our experience, or a fact experienced by us. We interpret it, and to some extent misinterpret it, as we do all other facts. If this partly true, and partly false, interpretation is what we mean by the word 'idea,' then it is the idea which is an inference from the being of our neighbour—an inference which can be checked by closer acquaintance—but we do not first have the idea of him, and then wonder whether a being, corresponding more or less to the idea, exists. If we had the idea of our fellow-beings first—before we had experience of them—if it were from the edge of the idea that we had to leap, we might reasonably doubt whether to fling ourselves into such a logical, or rather into such an illogical, abyss. But it is from their being as an experienced fact, that we start; and with the intention of constructing from it as logical an idea as lies within our power. What is inference is not the being but the idea, so far as the idea is thus constructed.

The idea, thus constructed, may be constructed correctly, or incorrectly. Whether it is constructed correctly or incorrectly is determined by further experience. What is important to notice is first that it is only by further experience, personal experience, that we can determine how far the construction we have put upon it is or is not correct; and, next, that so far as the construction we have put upon it is correct, that is to say is confirmed by actual experience, it is thereby shown to be not inference—even though it was reached by a process of inference—but fact. The process of inference may be compared to a path by which we struggle up the face of a cliff: it is the path by which we get there, but it is not the firm ground on which eventually we rest. The path is not that which upholds the cliff; nor is the inference that on which the being of God rests. The being of God is not something inferred but something experienced. It is by experience—the experience of ourselves or others—that we find out whether what by inference we were led to expect is really something of which we can—if we will—have experience. And that which is experienced ceases, the moment it is experienced, to be inferential. The experience is fact: the statement of it in words is truth. But apart from the experience, the words in which it is stated are but words; and, without the experience, the words must remain for ever words and nothing more than words.

If then by the idea of God we mean the words, in which it is (inadequately) stated, and nothing more, the idea of God is separated by an impassable gulf from the being of God. Further, if we admit that the idea is, by its very nature, and by the very facts of the case, essentially different from the being of God, then it is of little use to continue to maintain that the being of God is a fact of human experience. In that case, the supposed fact of experience is reduced to something of which we neither have, nor can have, any idea, or consciousness, whatever. It thereby ceases to be a fact of experience at all. And it is precisely on this assumption that the being of God is denied to be a fact of experience—the assumption that being and idea are separated from one another by an impassable gulf: the idea we can be conscious of, but of His being we can have no experience. We must therefore ask not whether this gulf is impassable, but whether it exists at all, or is of the same imaginary nature as that to which Gloucester was led by Edgar.

That there may be beings, of whom we have no idea, is a proposition which it is impossible to disprove. Such beings would be *ex hypothesi* no part of our experience; and if God were such a being, man would have no experience of Him. And, having no experience of Him, man could have no idea of Him. But the experience man has, of those beings whom he knows, is an experience in which idea and being are given together. Even if in thought we attend to one rather than to the other of the two aspects, the idea is still the idea of the being; and the being is still the being of the idea. So far from there being an impassable gulf between the two, the two are inseparable, in the moment of actual experience. It is in moments of reflection that they appear separable and separate, for the memory remains, when the actual experience has ceased. We have then only to call the memory the idea, and then the idea, in this use of the word, is as essentially different from that of which it is said to be the idea, as the memory of a being or thing is from the being or thing itself. If we put the memory into words, and pronounce those words to another, we communicate to him what we remember of our experience (modified—perhaps transmogrified—by our reflections upon it) but we do not communicate the actual experience, simply because we cannot. What we communicate may lead him to actual experience for himself; but it is not itself the experience. The memory may give rise, in ourselves or in others to whom we communicate, to expectation and anticipation; and the expectation is the more likely to be realised, the less the memory has been transmogrified by reflection. But, both the memory and the anticipation are clearly different from actual experience. It is only when they are confused with one aspect of the actual experience—that which we have called the idea—that the idea is supposed to be detachable from the being of whom we have actual experience. The idea is part of the experience; the memory obviously is not.

If then it be said that the being of God is always an inference and is never anything more, the reply is that the being of anything whatever that is remembered or expected is, in the moment of memory or of anticipation, inferential; but, in the moment of actual experience, it is not inferred—it is experienced. And what is experienced is, and from the beginning has always been, in religions of the lower as well as of the higher culture, at once the being and the idea of God.

INDEX

www.ingramcontent.com/pod-product-compliance
Ingram Content Group UK Ltd.
Pitfield, Milton Keynes, MK11 3LW, UK
UKHW042144280225
455719UK00001B/82

9 781107 634602